WATER WON'T QUENCH THE FIRE

Sermons For Sundays
After Pentecost (First Third)
Cycle B, Gospel Texts

William G. Carter

CSS Publishing Company, Inc., Lima, Ohio

WATER WON'T QUENCH THE FIRE

Library of Congress Cataloging-in-Publication Data

Carter, William G., 1960-
    Water won't quench the fire : sermons for Sundays after Pentecost (first third) : cycle
B, Gospel texts / William G. Carter.
        p.   cm.
    ISBN 0-7880-0797-1 (pbk.)
    1. Presbyterian Church—United States—Sermons. 2. Sermons, American. 3. Bible.
N.T. Gospels—Sermons. 4. Church year sermons. I. Title.
BX9178.C35W37   1996
252'.6—dc20   96-4985
                                                                            CIP

Dedicated

to Edgar Frank,
    who invoked my awe of the Almighty
    and always remembered my birthday,

to Sheldon Seibel,
    who pointed me toward God's kingdom, on earth as
        in heaven,
    and showed me that real pastors wear blue jeans,

to John Mahler,
    who prompted my faith in Jesus Christ
    and awakened my understanding through well-told
        stories,

and to Mom and Dad,
    who gave me the opportunity to sit in a pew
    and listen to the Gospel these three pastors
        proclaimed.

Table Of Contents

Foreword by Thomas G. Long   **7**

Introduction: Subverted By Grace   **9**

Day Of Pentecost   **13**
Learning To Live Without Jesus
John 15:26-27; 16:4b-15 (C)

Day Of Pentecost   **21**
Water Won't Quench The Fire
John 7:37-39 (L)

Day Of Pentecost   **27**
A Blessing Behind Locked Doors
John 20:19-23 (RC)

Holy Trinity   **33**
A Breeze In The Dark
John 3:1-17 (C, L)

Holy Trinity   **39**
Sent From The Mountain
Matthew 28:16-20 (RC)

Corpus Christi   **47**
A Taste Of Life
Mark 14:12-16, 22-26 (RC)

Proper 4   **55**
Pentecost 2
Ordinary Time 9
Can Christians Dance?
Mark 2:23—3:6 (C, RC)
Mark 2:23-28 (L)

Proper 5   **61**
Pentecost 3
Ordinary Time 10
    Looking A Little Bit Crazy
    Mark 3:20-35

Proper 6   **69**
Pentecost 4
Ordinary Time 11
    How To Plant An English Garden
    Mark 4:26-34

Proper 7   **75**
Pentecost 5
Ordinary Time 12
    Shouting At A Storm
    Mark 4:35-41

Proper 8   **83**
Pentecost 6
Ordinary Time 13
    Time Taken, Life Restored
    Mark 5:21-43

Proper 9   **89**
Pentecost 7
Ordinary Time 14
    Anybody Listening?
    Mark 6:1-13 (C)
    Mark 6:1-6 (L, RC)

Lectionary Preaching After Pentecost   **97**

C — Revised Common Lectionary; RC — Roman Catholic Lectionary; L — Lutheran Lectionary

Foreword

There is an air of unpredictability about William G. Carter's sermons. One can never tell where he will take us or what we will see. We may find ourselves shining a flashlight into the bushes searching for wayward teenagers at a summer church camp, rushing down a hospital corridor with a minister improbably dressed as a clown as he hastens to the bedside of a child, or trying to make sense of a "You don't have to be crazy to work here, but it helps" sign hanging over a church secretary's desk.

Improbable characters and artifacts turn up all over the place: a nursing home resident abandoning her walker to dance the polka, an expert on English gardens clicking off slides at a club luncheon, cows listlessly chewing their cuds beneath a Jesus-is-coming sign along the highway. This volume is an attic full of eccentric treasures ready for a rainy day's exploring.

In short, these sermons are an eruption of ingenious images, powerful experiences, and inventive connections. In order to understand their genesis, it helps to know that Bill Carter is a gifted jazz pianist for whom the unexpected riff, the improbable chord is the nature of the art. But, true to jazz form, underneath the surprises is a steady beat. There are unpredictabilities here, astonishments, jump starts to the imagination, but they all rest on a trustworthy foundation. The unexpected pleasures of these sermons are the product of a solid biblical interpretation performed by the writer's keen and reliable theological mind. The result of this interplay of creativity and fidelity is that these sermons are a splash of wildflowers growing in a rich and loamy soil. Like the superb composer that he is, Bill Carter leads us deep into unexplored territory, but, no matter how far he takes us, finally he always brings us home.

So, relax and enjoy these sermons. Enjoy their humor, their joyful interplay of the biblical and the contemporary, their delightful poetic cadences. But do not be lulled into inattentiveness. Just when we tip back our chair and settle in to listen to the music, the rhythms seize us and we suddenly realize that we are being beckoned not to tap our feet on the sidelines but to get out of our seats and dance.

Thomas G. Long
Princeton Theological Seminary
Princeton, New Jersey

Introduction: Subverted by Grace

I was baptized on March 19, 1961, at North Springfield Presbyterian Church in Akron, Ohio. It was not, as far as I can tell, a memorable occasion. My parents were nervous and young, relatively untutored in the finer points of liturgical theology. They lived in a nearby trailer park, and felt no hurry to baptize their firstborn son. According to the official records, my father himself was not in a rush. He was baptized in the minister's study about thirty minutes before the worship service. "First things first," Rev. Duffy told him.

Whatever the case, it was no big deal to baptize babies and their parents in 1961. Baptism looked like a general endorsement of our membership in American culture. It was similar to receiving a birth certificate or a Social Security number. Baptism was an all-too-brief initiation rite into a country full of apparently Christian people who generally assented to Christian beliefs. Post-war optimism and the Baby Boom reinforced the mood. I was one of four male infants baptized on that March morning, and many more children were scheduled. A new Christian Education building had recently been built by the vigorous congregation to accommodate me and my peers. The sanctuary was packed each week by people who came to hear cheerful sermons. Folks in Akron still regard that time as the golden era of North Springfield church.

We didn't know we were living under the illusion of American Christendom. Even though most Protestant churches were bustling at the time, we soon found ourselves entangled in Vietnam, saw our heroes assassinated by fellow citizens, and watched our cities deteriorate. We lost our innocence. By the end of the decade, any equating of Akron or anywhere else with the Holy City was exposed as a dashed hope.

Yet the Christian church still baptizes people young and old. Maybe that's because baptism never intends to make anybody a good American; rather, Christian baptism announces our membership in God's kingdom. There is a profound distinction between the two citizenships. Baptism drowns us to the false powers of this age, and signifies we are brought alive by the power of the Risen Christ. A baptized person is given the means to see life differently through the lens of God's activity in Jesus Christ.

When Jesus was baptized, the Gospel of Mark says the heavens were ripped open and a whole new age began. God announced his claim on Jesus, and sent the Holy Spirit to fill him with the power to discern and serve. The same pattern holds for those of us who have been baptized in the name of Jesus. The Holy One announces we belong to God before we belong to anybody else. God sends the Spirit to help us discern what it means to belong to the reign of God, and fills us with the power to serve accordingly. We are gathered by the *water* of baptism and commissioned by the *fire* of the Holy Spirit. Water won't quench this fire.

As an infant, I couldn't know that my baptism initiated me into God's new dominion. The church had to teach me the truth. My instruction took place in worship services that sometimes seemed endless, Sunday School classes both delightful and dull, youth group retreats full of boiling adolescent hormones, and committee meetings that frequently appeared pointless. Nevertheless God got through. Like John Calvin, conversion did not come as a blinding flash that knocked me off my horse. My conversion began in baptism, and continued with the growing awareness that God had given me a "teachable heart."

There were special illuminations along the way, offering brief glimpses of another age already at hand. Like some of the stories you will encounter in this book, they sneaked up on me as the Holy Spirit gave eyes to see and ears to hear. I recall, for instance, a joyful funeral with a widow in a bright red hat, potluck dinners that made companions of strangers, church softball games that ended with tied scores and everybody winning, rousing hymns that provoked me to tune up with the saints, and, to get to the point, preachers who spoke as if something was at stake. I fondly recall the three pastors listed in the dedication as bold heralds of good news. Their sermons became the main course for many Sunday dinners at my parents' table. Together we chewed on our preachers' insights and found nourishment in their weekly offerings. Left to my own devices, my life would be even more prone to selfishness and self-preservation than it already is. Thanks to God, I have been subverted by grace, and gathered into Christ's regime of justice, mercy, and sacrificial love.

That, if anything, is what these sermons are all about: God's ceaseless attempt to undermine our illusions and gather us into a whole new kingdom. A collection of sermons is inevitably episodic, especially if the lectionary is the only thread that strings them together. Yet I pray that God will stitch together something useful from the scraps I've collected here.

No pastor preaches in a vacuum. I am grateful to the people of the First Presbyterian Church of Clarks Summit, for whom these sermons were composed. In every way these wonderful folks live as if God rules over heaven and earth. They take the Gospel seriously and practice it joyfully. They expect good preaching and remain gracious when I do not deliver it.

Four good friends have enriched my life with their gifts. Guy Griffith and Linda Williams make themselves available any time of day or night, and, despite my best intentions, they refuse to let me grow pompous and overstuffed. I am thankful for Tom Long, who wrote the foreword and taught me how to preach, and who, in the minds of Guy and Linda, is far too generous with his kind words for my work. Special thanks also go to saxophonist Al Hamme, who frequently hires me to play piano with his jazz bands, thus filling my life with something more than church work.

Three colleagues have been particularly helpful. Nancy Owens tends to the details of my professional life, so that I can tend to my crazy dreams. She is faithful in matters great and small, vigilant over potential distractions, and an efficient partner in Christ's work. I would be lost without her. Jamie Urso has been a source of support and sunshine from the beginning of this project. She is a first-class typist, a trusted friend, and the very picture of God's activity in a person's life. The Rev. Barbara Muntzel is a valued colleague in pastoral ministry. Barb assessed many of these sermons in the chancel when she thought nobody else was looking. Her frequent "thumb's up" behind the communion table provides welcome encouragement.

My greatest praise is for the three females in the Carter household. Colleen Lane Carter, my wife, polishes the tarnish from my ideas and sweeps the cobwebs from my soul. She is an engaging companion, an excellent editor, a talented riding instructor, and a wonderful mom. In the words of Wendell Berry, we share "no little economy based on the exchange of my love and work for yours."

Katherine Ann Carter, child of the covenant, takes delight in life, music, and chatty conversation. She provides us with constant joy and inspiration. Thanks, Kate, for inviting me to tell you a "Jesus story" every night before bedtime.

Our daughter Margaret Rose Carter was born while this book was still being midwifed. Meg will be baptized soon. Before her brow is dry, we intend to tell her about her new "crazy cousins," her gracious single Parent in heaven, and the new life made possible through Jesus Christ our Lord. "Your baptism matters a great deal," we'll say. And water won't quench the fire.

William G. Carter
Clarks Summit, Pennsylvania

Learning to Live
Without Jesus

Everywhere you looked, you saw people in tie-dyed t-shirts. Mothers gave drinks of apple juice to their children, while men in gray pigtails sipped Budweiser and tossed the empties beneath somebody's car. Teenagers spread blankets on the asphalt and took naps in the summer sunshine. Middle-aged hippies danced freely throughout the Philadelphia parking lot. Hundreds of mourners spontaneously gathered outside the Spectrum to bid goodbye to rock guitarist Jerry Garcia.

Whenever Jerry Garcia and the Grateful Dead came trucking into Philadelphia, the Spectrum was their preferred arena for concerts. They played some fifty concerts at the Spectrum. So it was a natural site for fans to gather when Garcia died of a heart attack in a California drug treatment facility. His music had gathered different generations in the same psychedelic experience. Under his influence, the Grateful Dead built a huge following by their live concerts, rather than through their infrequent recordings. They stood free from the star-making machinery of the music business. They made music about joy, peace, and spontaneity, and large numbers of weary, stressed-out, buttoned-down Baby Boomers found freedom and consolation in their tunes.

"We just feel like it's the end of an era," a New Jersey fan said. "We're not lost. Our life is not ending, but it was such a good thing." Then someone else added, "I don't know how we're going to live without Jerry."[1]

Whether or not we know Jerry Garcia and his music, most of us know how difficult it is to say good-bye to a hero. Those of us who belong to the church can be especially sympathetic. For, in a far more profound sense, we too have lost a loved one who has been the center of our lives, the source of our joy, the wellspring of our celebration. Each week we gather in the name of a leader who is not here. And whether or not we realize it, our Christian faith is the attempt to answer the question, "How are we going to live without Jesus?"

Now, somebody will probably say, "Wait! Jesus hasn't gone anywhere. He is still present with his church. He's right here, present in our hearts." That certainly sounds like a cozy thing to say. But how dare we say it? A young father tried to hush an exuberant young daughter who stomped around a church sanctuary on a weekday afternoon. "Please be quiet. This is God's house." With that, the curious girl pushed open the sanctuary door, peered around, and then announced, "Don't worry. God's not home today."

The text we heard this morning reminds us that the fundamental crisis of the church was the departure of Jesus. He is the source of our lives, like the vine beneath so many branches. We did not choose Jesus; he chose us, and appointed us to be faithful followers. Yet he is gone. That is what Easter means. "He is risen," the angel said, "and *he is not here.*" Easter faith tries to make sense of that absence.

The New Testament writer who deals most with this issue is the writer of John. In the fourth Gospel, Jesus speaks at length with his disciples before his death and resurrection. He washes their feet on his last night with them. He tells them at length that he is leaving them. He prays for them before he returns to the Father. Then comes the actual departure. As Fred Craddock says in his commentary on John, "Before the departing Christ, the disciples had been as children playing on the floor, only to look up and see the parents putting on coats and hats. The questions are three (and they have not changed): Where are you going? Can we go? Then who is going to stay with us?"[2]

Where are you going? "I am going to the Father and you will see me no longer" (John 16:10).

Can we go? "Where I am going, you cannot come" (John 13:33).

Then who will stay with us? "When the Advocate comes, whom I will send to you from the Father, the Spirit of Truth who comes from the Father, he will testify on my behalf" (John 15:26).

How are we going to live without Jesus? The answer, according to the Gospel of John, lies in the presence of the Holy Spirit. John calls him the Spirit of Truth, the Advocate, the Paraclete. In the absence of Jesus, his presence draws near to his followers. If he had not left us, the Spirit would not have come. Since Jesus has departed once and for all, he can now come and dwell with us through the presence of another Advocate.

Admittedly this sounds like double-talk to a lot of people, both inside and outside of the church. It is difficult to talk about the Holy Spirit. Outside the church, whenever people talk about a person's spirit continuing on, they usually point to those people left behind who hold the same values as their hero and who extend the impact of what their hero did or said. After Jerry Garcia died, for instance, an MTV interviewer pointed a camera in the face of somebody in San Francisco. "How are you handling the news of Garcia's death?" she asked. "Jerry's music lives on, man! His spirit will always be with us." To which the interviewer added, "Like, wow, man! Right on!" To translate: we may never get rid of the sixties. Some of that decade's values continue to fill the air like a thick green smoke.

Inside the church, we find it hard to talk about the Spirit of Jesus. It's easy to say, "Jesus has left us and his Spirit is here," but that doesn't necessarily mean we hold his values or extend his impact. Sensing a spiritual void, the church frequently turns to more administrative matters.

In a regional office of my denomination, an official-looking flyer appeared on at least seven different bulletin boards. Did it announce a prayer meeting? A Bible study? An ecumenical worship service? No. It was a memo warning the employees not to let stray paper clips fall on the carpet. "The last time somebody dropped a

15

paper clip on the floor," the memo stated, "a vacuum cleaner ran over it and broke down. We spent hundreds of dollars by needlessly repairing our vacuum cleaner."

Given such a memo, and the issue that prompted it, you really begin to wonder about the church's wasted resources. We live in a world that ignores both its Creator and its creatures, a world that peddles sound bytes as treatises of fact, a world that deceitfully tells us that we can make ourselves righteous if only we keep trying harder. In short, our world hungers to know the grace and truth of Jesus Christ. Meanwhile the church is preoccupied with paper clips on its own bureaucratic floor.

We struggle in the church to wait for the Spirit, to be led by the Spirit, to live by the Spirit who has many things to tell us that we cannot yet bear to hear. It is difficult to wait for a Spirit whom we cannot touch or see. No wonder, then, that sometimes in our impatience we turn to flesh and blood. We turn to the church for undue authority, expecting a list of what we should and should not do. Either that, or the church itself fills the absence of Jesus with its own false certainty and pretends it has all the answers.

A pastor I know tells of a horrifying experience in a Christian bookstore. She was looking for a commentary on the book of Deuteronomy when a man with an earnest face approached her. "How are you doing, sister? Isn't this a beautiful day the Lord has made? Praise the Lord! Let's say Amen together." She ignored him.

Unfortunately that made things worse. He began to pay attention to her. He said, "Maybe you didn't hear me when I said, 'Praise the Lord!' Listen, sister, I want to hear you say a good word for Jesus." He continued to annoy her. Finally she turned to him and said, "I'm the pastor at Central Presbyterian Church. I'm shopping for a Bible commentary. When I find the book I'm looking for, I will use it to write a sermon in which I will say a lot of good words for Jesus. In the meantime, please leave me alone."

"You can't be a pastor," he said. "My Bible won't allow women to be pastors." She reached into her wallet, pulled out a business card, and handed it to him. Then she turned back to her shopping. "No, listen," he said, "the Bible doesn't say anything about women becoming preachers. You're wrong. Your whole life is a sin."

"Well," she replied, "why don't we let the Holy Spirit decide, since it was the Holy Spirit who called me into the ministry? In the meantime, I found my book and I'm going to pay for it now. Good-bye."

"I can't let you go yet," he said. "Your salvation is at stake. You're a woman and you don't know your place. Worse than that, you don't know the Bible. I'm worried about your soul. If you should die tonight, you would go to hell. I would be held accountable if I didn't tell you the truth."

By this point, dying wouldn't have been so bad. At least she would have been free of silly fools in Christian bookstores. Somehow she found the strength to speak to him. She said, "If you're so concerned with truth, let me tell you what I know. In life and death, I belong to God. God called me to serve him, regardless of whether or not that's written down in your Bible. My 'place' was choosing to obey him. I believe the Holy Spirit led me into this truth, and I trust the Holy Spirit will sort it out." Then she added, "As far as hell is concerned, that is God's decision, not mine nor yours. If it were up to me, hell would be full of people who cling to a Bible they never think about, and heaven would be full of people who trust in a God they cannot see."

Christian faith is just that: faith in Christ. We trust what we have heard him say through scripture, yet we remain open to hear him still speak through the Holy Spirit. In the end, we trust God will sort everything out, for the primary role of the Spirit is to point to Jesus and guide us into his truth. The Spirit of Christ will lead us into the life that Christ has come to give. The Spirit will teach us; the question is whether we are willing to learn.

What is required is a new openness to the Spirit. God is free to speak, even if the words are not yet written down in our ancient Bibles. God is able to save the world, far beyond our capacity to manage the paper clips. Faith requires us to remain open to any act of God. That, it seems to me, is how we live without Jesus. That is how we live by the Holy Spirit. Like the wind, the Spirit blows when and where it wills. We have no control over what God is doing in the world. But if we open our arms like a cross-mast, if we set our sails and wait for the Spirit to blow and propel us, we find ourselves directed into the deep waters of grace.

17

It is difficult to trust God like that. Sometimes it is easier to look elsewhere for our security and approval. Like the day when Charlie Brown stopped at the psychiatric help stand to talk with Lucy. He confesses, "My trouble is I never know if I'm doing the right thing. I need to have someone around who can tell me when I'm doing the right thing." Lucy says, "Okay. You're doing the right thing. That'll be five cents, please!" Charlie Brown walks away with a smile on his face.

In a few minutes, he returns with a frown. "Back already?" asks Lucy. "What happened?" Charlie Brown says, "I was wrong. It didn't help. You need more in life than just having someone around to tell you when you're doing the right thing." Lucy says, "Now you've really learned something! That'll be another five cents please."[3]

"When the Spirit of truth comes," said Jesus, "he will guide you into all the truth." That is the instruction we need, and that is what Christ promises. If the world grows deaf and blind to its Creator, the Spirit says, "All things were created through him, and without him not one thing came into being" (John 1:3). If the world confuses you with tempting alternatives, the Spirit says, "I am the light of the world. Whoever follows me will never walk in darkness but will have the light of life" (John 8:12). If the world hates you, mistreats you, abuses you, the Spirit says, "The world hated me before it hated you . . . and I have chosen you out of the world" (John 15:18-19). If the world tells you that you are all alone, cut off from all help and strength, the Spirit says, "I am the vine, you are the branches. Those who abide in me and I in them bear much fruit, because apart from me you can do nothing" (John 15:5).

"When the Spirit of truth comes," Jesus said, "he will testify on my behalf." And if we remain open to that Spirit, we may discover that, even in his absence, Jesus has been with us all along.

---

1. Suzanne Sataline and Jemele Hill, "Fans ponder their world without him," *The Philadelphia Inquirer* 10 August 1995: A1.

2. Fred B. Craddock, *John* (Atlanta: John Knox Press, 1982), p. 98.

3. Robert L. Short, *Short Meditations on the Bible and Peanuts* (Louisville: Westminster/John Knox Press, 1990), pp. 45-46.

Water Won't
Quench The Fire

An unusual piece of mail arrived at the office the other day. Inside the envelope was a colorful brochure, a response card, and a prepaid business reply envelope. A computer-generated cover letter was addressed to First Presbyterian Church.

"Dear First," it began, "have you ever found yourself in deep spiritual need? Are you hungry for meaning in your life? Would you like to free yourself from earthly constrictions and reach for the light of perfect bliss? If so, Mr. Church, then you and the whole Church family can try a new audiocassette program titled *The Higher Being*. It is yours to audition free for the next thirty days. If these tapes convince you that you can find perfect fulfillment, you can keep them for only $39.95, $20.00 off the regular price. If you don't find Infinite Peace through these tapes, return them and owe nothing. VISA and MasterCard accepted."

Every church office receives more than its share of spiritual junk mail. Somebody is always trying to sell the newest Bible study programs, the most successful prayer manual, or the latest design of plastic communion cups. These days there are hundreds of opportunities for church people to buy religious merchandise. Christian marketing firms have baptized materialism in an effort to make a buck. Yet this slick brochure stood out from all the rest. Was it an innocent marketing mix-up or a wrong address on someone's database? It struck me as something far more devilish.

21

Whoever was selling those tapes was peddling fulfillment, freedom, meaning, and peace. The church has always claimed these things are not for sale.

Perhaps it is a symptom of our age to think we can fill a spiritual vacuum by listening to one more tape, reading one more book, or giving our money to one more guru. A young woman told me about dropping by a health food store not long ago. I don't know why she was there; most of the foods she eats are not very healthy. But there she was, among the racks of herbal teas and natural fibers. After thumbing through some compact disks of Celtic harp music, she spotted a book section marked "spirituality." That looked interesting, until she read the titles of the books. There were books about esoteric crystals and secret pyramids. One book offered tips on getting in touch with past lives. Another suggested ways to interpret dreams. There wasn't a Bible to be seen. There were no books on prayer or studies on the Sermon on the Mount. A sales clerk said, "Have you found what you're looking for?"

"Not exactly," she replied.

"Well, we're proud of our section on spirituality," the clerk said. "We do our best to keep up with the latest ideas."

That seems to describe the current fad for spirituality. Here in America, people are perpetually hungry for something new. With all of the current talk about spirituality in our culture, the church is in an awkward position. The church keeps offering the same old thing, and his name is Jesus Christ.

In the text we heard today, Jesus says, "Let anyone who is thirsty come to me." There is nothing new or novel about his words. He simply invites people to come and drink, to taste and see if he can truly quench their thirsts.

As Raymond Brown notes in his commentary on John, it is ironic that Jesus issues his invitation on the Feast of Tabernacles. The Feast of Tabernacles, or Succoth, took place in late September or early October. It began as a harvest festival, but by the time of the prophet Zechariah, the feast had become an occasion to pray for rain. The feast was so important, said the prophet, that if a family did not go to Jerusalem for the Feast of Tabernacles, God would not send any rain upon them in the coming year (Zechariah

14:17). To symbolize the "living waters" which God would provide, during every day of the seven-day feast the priest would lead a procession down the hill from the Temple to the fountain of Gihon. He would fill a golden pitcher with water. Then the procession would turn around and climb the hill to the altar, where the priest would pour the water through a silver funnel into the ground.[1]

On the seventh and greatest day of the Feast, Jesus pointed to himself and said, "If anyone is thirsty, let them come to me and drink." These are radical words, for Jesus strips away all the trappings of tradition. He judges every religious practice that does not point to him. Beyond the rituals, the holy days, and the temple liturgies, Jesus points to himself as the One who satisfies our deepest craving. The Gospel of John claims the one human desire is to know God, to taste God, for that is the essence of life. If the primary human craving is a thirst for God, it will not be quenched through cassette tapes on human potential or self-fulfillment seminars. The heart of Christian spirituality is taking in Jesus Christ through faith. He is the source of our life and strength.

In *The Silver Chair,* one of C. S. Lewis' Chronicles of Narnia, there is a scene where a young girl named Jill meets Aslan the Lion. Jill is "dreadfully thirsty," and she sees a stream bright as glass. Beside it lay the Lion, the Christ figure, who says, "If you're thirsty, you may drink." Jill stands frozen in fear. The Lion asks her, "Are you not thirsty?"

> "I'm dying of thirst," said Jill.
> "Then drink," said the Lion.
> "May I — could I — would you mind going away while I do?" said Jill.
> The Lion answered this only by a look and a very low growl. And as Jill gazed at its motionless bulk, she realized that she might as well have asked the whole mountain to move aside for her convenience.
> The delicious rippling noise of the stream was driving her nearly frantic.
> "Will you promise not to do anything to me, if I do come?" said Jill.

"I make no promise," said the Lion.

Jill was so thirsty now that, without noticing it, she had come a step nearer.

"Do you eat girls?" she said.

"I have swallowed up girls and boys, women and men, kings and emperors, cities and realms," said the Lion. It didn't say this as if it were boasting, nor as if it were sorry, nor as if it were angry. It just said it.

"I daren't come and drink," said Jill.

"Then you will die of thirst," said the Lion.

"Oh dear!" said Jill, coming another step nearer. "I suppose I must go and look for another stream then."

"There is no other stream," said the Lion.

It never occurred to Jill to disbelieve the Lion — no one who had seen his stern face could do that — and her mind suddenly made itself up. It was the worst thing she ever had to do, but she went forward to the stream, knelt down, and began scooping up water in her hand. It was the coldest, most refreshing water she had ever tasted. You didn't need to drink much of it, for it quenched your thirst at once.[2]

The promise of the gospel is that we have access to a water like this as we believe in Jesus Christ. As we trust him with our lives, we participate in the very life of the Eternal One. That is the meaning of the phrase "eternal life." According to the Gospel of John, eternal life is not merely a dwelling place in heaven where we go when we die; it is a quality of life that we can claim here and now. This is the life of God himself, the very Breath of creation. We can call it living water. Or we can call it the Holy Spirit. Whatever we call it, it is a gift of life, given to us through faith, and it cannot be defeated by death.

Even so, this does not mean that Christian spirituality is merely a weekly return to the heavenly watering trough. For the person who is "in Christ," life is meant to be expressed and shared. Perhaps that is the reason for a delightful ambiguity within our text. Jesus says, "Within him shall flow rivers of living water." But it is not clear whom he is talking about. Is Jesus saying, in effect, that a river runs through him? Perhaps. As he says elsewhere in this gospel, "The water that I will give will become a spring of water gushing up to eternal life" (John 4:14). Maybe that is why the writer of the Gospel of John focuses our gaze on a particular event that happened at the cross. A soldier pierced the body of Jesus with a spear and "water came out from his side" (John 19:34-35). From within the crucified and glorified Lord, there flows the water of life.

Yet the passage could also be translated as it appears in the New Revised Standard Version: "Out of the believer's heart shall flow rivers of living water." There is no punctuation in Greek text, so we are left to ponder what Jesus is talking about. Does living water come from Jesus? Yes, it does. Does living water flow from within the believer's heart? Yes, it can. For this is the clearest expression of the mystery of Christian spirituality: We drink our life from Jesus, and the living water spills out of us to others. We cannot hoard Christ or keep him to ourselves. If we truly take him in through faith, the promise is that he will flow through us to others. His risen life infuses our lives. Through us, his life extends into the life of the world.

After Hugh Kerr retired from a distinguished teaching career at Princeton Theological Seminary, he moved to a small apartment in a retirement community. To pass the time, he continued to write articles and read books. He also volunteered to deliver mail. One day he was delivering letters in the health care clinic attached to the community. A black woman attendant was playing "Amazing Grace" on the piano in the social room. She did not seem to be a schooled musician for the notes, rhythms, and variations were very much her own. She played in a kind of broken ragtime, a bit slow and deliberate. Now and then she punctuated the words of the hymn with her own phrase, "Praise God, Praise God."

Hugh noticed how nurses, volunteers, and maintenance people passed by detached and uninterested. Few seemed to notice there was something within that woman that was spilling over into the room, a river of life, a means of grace and truth. Hugh stood and listened for a few minutes. Then he caught the piano player's eye, and said a quiet "thank you." In that moment, in that woman, he said, "I discerned the presence of Christ."[3]

Ever since Easter, the word is out that Jesus Christ is alive. If he draws near to us, his presence is not immediately obvious. Yet every now and then, God lifts the veil, giving us a glimpse of Christ in the gentle word or generous gift, in the compassionate deed or the joyful song. Jesus Christ is alive; and as his first order of business, he comes to fill us with life. His gracious, abundant life promises to spill into every parched, weary heart, until the day when even a dying world will be raised from the dead. That is the intent of Christ's living water, promised in Easter and sealed in the fire of Pentecost. And water won't quench the fire.

---

1. Raymond E. Brown, *The Gospel According to John I-XII* (Garden City, NY: Doubleday & Company, Inc., 1966), pp. 326-327.

2. C. S. Lewis, *The Silver Chair* (New York: HarperCollins *Publishers* Limited, Collier Books, 1970), pp. 15-18. Used by permission.

3. Hugh T. Kerr, "Discerning the Presence," *Theology Today* 44.3 (October 1987), p. 305.

A Blessing
Behind Locked Doors

Every Sunday morning, the people of a church in the Pacific Northwest say, "Peace be with you." They begin the worship service with a hymn of praise. The people confess their sins together, and hear of God's forgiveness. Then they are invited to turn to others around them and pass the peace. It has become an exuberant moment in an otherwise sober occasion. Friends leave their pews to embrace one another. Newcomers are warmly welcomed with a kind word or a hug.

Nobody thought much about the weekly ritual until the pastor received a letter from a man who had recently joined the congregation. The new member was a promising young lawyer from a prestigious downtown law firm. He drafted a brief but pointed letter on his firm's letterhead. "I am writing to complain about the congregational ritual known as 'passing the peace,' " he wrote. "I disagree with it, both personally and professionally, and I am prepared to take legal action to cause this practice to cease." When the pastor phoned to talk with the lawyer about the letter, he asked why the man was so disturbed. The lawyer said, "The passing of the peace is an invasion of my privacy."

Perhaps that story could only happen in the 1990s. These are strange times. I have no doubt that there are people who would take their church to court if too many people shook their hands, or if neighbors were too friendly, or if fellow pewsitters interrupted

27

their private little religious moments. To that end, I think the pastor's response to the lawyer was right on target. He said, "Like it or not, when you joined the church you gave up some of your privacy, for we believe in a risen Lord who will never leave us alone." Then he added, "You never know when Jesus Christ will intrude on us with a word of peace."

That's exactly what happened in today's Easter story from the twentieth chapter of John. The disciples were huddled in Jerusalem, recovering from the trauma of Jesus' death. The writer tells us the doors of the house were locked out of fear. Suddenly the Lord appeared to them and said, "Peace be with you." He showed them the nail prints in his hands and feet, the sword wound in his side. With no small joy, the disciples realized the crucified Jesus had become the Risen Lord. Then, for a second time, Christ said, "Peace be with you."

Since they had been cowering in a corner, Jesus could have said a number of things that might have been more helpful. He might have said, "Look, it's me; I was dead, but now I live." Or he could have said, "Pilate and my enemies did not have the last word on my life; God is stronger than every power that can hurt or destroy." Instead his word to them was, "Peace be with you." He greeted them with a message of blessing and good cheer. The word of peace was the last message the disciples expected to hear.

No doubt they had locked the doors because of what happened to the Messenger. Two days before, Jesus had died and was buried. His closest followers knew their own lives were in danger. Now here he was on Sunday night, somehow alive again, inescapably present in their midst. That must have been a shock. They had heard second-hand reports that Jesus had been raised from the dead. Yet it's one thing to hear the news. It's another thing to see a dead friend who had come back to life. No wonder they were terrified.

No doubt they considered keeping the doors locked because of how Jesus commissioned them. The Risen Christ came and said, "As the Father sent me, so do I send you." That's quite a challenge. As he gave his life, they were required to give their lives: to reveal a loving God to a hostile world, to speak truthful words to a deceitful generation, to wash the feet of a soiled church. Just like Jesus, the disciples were called to lay down their lives for their friends, and speak as witnesses for eternal life in the face of certain death.

The greatest challenge for the disciples was not embracing the resurrected Lord. Nor did they deny the open commission he gave them. Rather, the continuing task that Jesus set before the church was to extend his simple greeting to others: "Peace be with you." Do we really want to pass the peace?

There's a church that said, "No, we don't want to do that." Their pastor tried to get them to change their minds, but she couldn't make it happen. Whenever the worship committee would get a new chairperson, she would pull the individual aside and say, "Our worship service flows pretty well. No major problems. There's only one little thing I think we should add. It's called 'passing the peace.' "

The first chairperson said, "I don't think so. I once visited a church that passed the peace. It got out of hand. People were leaving their pews, wandering up and down the aisles, hugging one another. Pure chaos! A stranger came up and hugged me and said 'Peace be with you.' I felt like slugging her. She was invading my space. We're not going to do that here."

A year later, a second chairperson took over. The pastor made her pitch. The lay leader said, "I never heard of such a thing. Where does the idea come from?" So the pastor gave him a brief history lesson. "According to church history," she said, "it became a weekly practice in worship by the year 604 A.D., at the time of Gregory the Great.[1] Before that, in the second century, Justin Martyr instructed the church to conclude the celebration of the Lord's Supper with a kiss of peace.[2] Prior to that, the apostle Paul wrote to the Romans and said, 'Greet one another with a holy kiss (Romans 16:16).' Around the world the church has been passing the peace for centuries."

The committee chair looked at her and said, "Well, it's a new idea around here. I don't think we should do it."

The following year, the pastor appointed a third chair for the committee and pleaded her case. By now, everybody on the worship committee knew of her efforts. With a single voice they said, "People come to church to hear about God; they don't come to be touched. Passing the peace isn't a holy moment. It is too informal, too human." Perhaps it is no surprise that the pastor now serves a different congregation.

Do we want to pass the peace? It is a practice that extends back to Jesus' first words to the disciples on the day of his resurrection. Nothing could be more human or more holy. Nothing could better express the ethical demand of the gospel.

According to the Gospel of John, Jesus gave his peace to people as he blew his spirit upon them. He did not impart the kind of peace that offers an absence of hassle or disturbance. Neither did he imply that his peace provides a quiet weekend away from the troubles of daily life. If anything, the peace of Christ is a gift of assurance in the thick of difficulty. It comes as a breath of life in the midst of sorrow and pain. As someone notes, "The peace of God is the confidence that God is God and neither our gains nor our losses are ultimate. It is the trust that God loves the world, is for all creatures, and is present with us in every endeavor to make real that love in concrete ways."[3]

What does it mean to pass the peace? First and foremost, it is a sign of forgiveness. The Risen Christ came to a fearful, unbelieving church that was scared of its own shadow, and his word promised to set all people free. He said, "If you forgive the sins of any, they are forgiven them; if you retain the sins of any, they are retained" (John 20:23). Jesus Christ charged his people to forgive, not because it is easy — it isn't — but because his people are witnesses of a merciful God whose very nature is to forgive.

In the wake of the first Rodney King trial, many of us watched Los Angeles explode in racial fury. Four white police officers had beaten Mr. King live on videotape. Two officers were acquitted by the court, and two others received short prison sentences. Los Angeles burned. Many senseless acts of violence were committed. One of those acts happened to a white truck driver named Reginald Denny. In April 1992, Denny was dragged from his cab and beaten by two black men. A camera caught that scene, too, and this time all the assailants were convicted and sentenced.

But something unusual happened during the trial. After giving his testimony in court, Reginald Denny shocked the judge, the jury, and the legal counsel when he came to the witness stand and embraced the mothers of his two assailants. He hugged the mothers of the men who had beaten him.

"I had to do it," he said. "The violence and the hatred has to stop somewhere. So why not have it stop with me?" It was a curious, Christ-like thing to do. Call it, if you will, an act of "passing the peace."

What does it mean to pass the peace? It is a sign of forgiveness, an indication that nothing can separate us from the love of God. More than that, it is also a sign that, in Christ, there is nothing that can separate us from the love of one another. When we pass the peace, we show our solidarity and support. Our gestures announce, "In the Risen Christ, God has stood for us, so today we stand with one another."

Some time ago, there was a newspaper story about Ian O'Gorman, an 11-year-old boy who was undergoing chemotherapy. Ian wasn't feeling well. Doctors discovered a tumor and removed it. They prescribed chemotherapy. He lost his hair. His classmates at Lake Elementary School wondered what they could do for Ian. They thought about making a large get-well card, and inviting people to sign their names. They considered pitching together and buying him flowers. They also prayed for his recovery, hoping for a miracle.

Yet they did something more. They shaved their heads. In one photograph, bald-headed Ian is surrounded by twelve friends who shaved their heads so he wouldn't feel out of place. Their teacher was so impressed that he shaved his head too. As one classmate explained, "We figured if everybody shaved their heads, people wouldn't know which one of us has cancer and which of us just shaved our heads."

A reporter asked, "Weren't you afraid that other kids would make fun of you when you shaved your heads?" "A little bit," said one kid, "because some of them made fun of Ian's looks. But Ian is our friend and we would do anything for him."[4] Of all the things they could have done for Ian, his classmates decided to pass the peace.

"Peace be with you." That's what Jesus says to fearful people of every age. The word of the Risen Christ has the power to unlock all kinds of doors. His spirit sends us into the world as he was sent: to reveal that the God who gave us breath shall fill us with peace. We are under obligation to make peace with one another.

"Peace be with you." Somebody may be waiting to hear those words from your lips. It might be a person in your home, at work, or among your acquaintances. Maybe it's a neighbor hurt by gossip, or a teacher whose innocence has been shattered by public opinion, or a child wounded by harsh judgment, or a middle-aged executive who is tongue-tied about his own emotions, or the person who still waits to hear a merciful word from your lips.

Today you could set somebody free. When the benediction is over, you could climb out of your pew, go to that person, and say, "Peace be with you." It is possible because Jesus Christ is risen. He is here among us, bearing a perfect love that casts out fear. He gives us the power to forgive and to stand with others.

So what are we going to do about it?

---

1. Aidan Kavanagh, *Elements of Rite: A Handbook of Liturgical Style* (New York: Pueblo Publishing Company, Inc., 1982), pp. 77-78.

2. Gilbert Cope, "Gestures," *The Westminster Dictionary of Worship* (Philadelphia: The Westminster Press, 1979), pp. 187-88.

3. Fred B. Craddock, *John* (Atlanta: John Knox Press, 1982), p. 111.

4. Richard Guentert, PresbyNet Sermonshop, as quoted from *The Des Moines Register* 3 March 1994.

A Breeze
In The Dark

In his autobiography, actor Alec Guinness tells a story that might
keep every pastor and church school teacher awake at night. He
was a teenager and it was the morning of his confirmation. The
classes were finished. The students' heads had been filled full of
Bible stories and theological doctrines. Guinness says Holy Trinity
Church in Eastbourne was crammed with confirmation candidates,
their parents, friends, schoolteachers, and sponsors.

At the appropriate moment, he notes, "The girls, mostly in grey
uniforms, filed up to kneel at the Bishop's left hand and the boys,
in blue serge, to his right. I remember white episcopal hands and
shaggy black eyebrows. A pale, greenish light filtered through the
window-panes, giving a subaqueous hue to the perspiring
congregation." Then he adds, "At the age of sixteen, one early
summer day, I arose from under the hands of the Bishop of Lewes
a confirmed atheist . . . With a flash I realized I had never really
believed what I had been taught."[1]

I don't know about you, but I am troubled by that story. I believe
in Christian education. God's people are called to teach the
Christian faith to children, teenagers, and adults. Sunday church
school and confirmation classes are important educational activities.
The church needs to do these things. And yet, here is the story of a
bright, intelligent person who emerged from those experiences,

and he did not believe a word of what he learned. As a professional church leader, as a Christian educator, that story bothers me.

At a personal level, however, that story haunts me for another reason, namely, that it sounds surprisingly familiar. On a bright Sunday morning, it is easy to affirm what we believe. As the familiar verse we've heard today puts it, "God so loved the world that he gave his only Son, so that everyone who believes in him may not perish but have eternal life." With sunbeams shining through stained glass, I can believe it. But late at night, after the lights are dimmed, sometimes I have my doubts, my questions, my lapses of belief.

Perhaps I'm not the only one. William Muehl, who taught at Yale Divinity School for many years, once noted how instructive it is to realize how many of the men and women in the pews almost did not come to church that morning. "In all probability," he writes, "most of them feel that they are there under false pretenses, that everyone around them feels more confidently Christian, less restlessly rebellious than they do themselves."[2]

The story of Nicodemus is the story of someone who struggles to believe. If you met him on the street during the day, you probably wouldn't have imagined it. Nicodemus was a Jew. He had a story of faith that stretched back to Father Abraham, who packed up a U-Haul and drove it across Mesopotamia because God told him to do so. Nicodemus was also a teacher of Israel, someone under obligation to tell the story of faith to others. And he was a leader of the Jews, a guiding force for the local synagogue, an influential person in the downtown Temple. What's more, he was a Pharisee, which meant he had gone through all the classes, learned all the Bible stories, and sat through all the ceremonies. Most importantly, Nicodemus knew the secret of the Gospel of John, that Jesus has come from God, that God's very presence dwells in him.

Yet even with all of his knowledge, something was missing. The writer says, "He came to Jesus by night." I don't know if we should take that literally or not. Certainly it was safer for Nicodemus the Pharisee to approach this upstart miracle worker after the sun went down. No one would see him lurking in the shadows. Few people would be awake to eavesdrop on their conversation. Yet it seems clear that when the writer says Nicodemus came "by night" he's not merely talking about the time of day. He is talking about a condition.

Later in this gospel, for instance, Jesus eats a meal with friends. The writer says the meal was a supper. As they were eating, Jesus turned to one of his friends, to someone he loved, and said, "Go and do what you have to do." Well, Judas kept the purse. Maybe he had to run to the market or make a Passover gift to the poor. But the writer of John tells us what Judas went out to do. After receiving the bread from Jesus, Judas went out to betray him. Then the writer adds the words, "And it was night" (John 13:30). Why does John say that? He has already implied that this event took place after supper. The writer wants us to know: Judas Iscariot, a beloved friend of Jesus, was in the dark.

Or even later, in chapter 19, a woman named Mary Magdalene stands at the foot of the cross of Jesus. She followed him even when all was lost. She stood there and watched him breathe his last breath. She was faithful even after others ran away. On the first day of the week, she went to the tomb. But the writer cues us, "It was still dark." As Mary discovered the empty tomb, she immediately thought the corpse had been stolen. Seeing two angels in dazzling white, she didn't fall down in fear, but began to cry. And when Jesus suddenly stood before her, she mistook him for the gardener. Why? Because "it was still dark" (John 20:1). Even those most faithful do not always understand.

According to the Fourth Gospel, "night" is more than a time of day. It is the condition of those who want to believe, yet, for one reason or another, cannot believe. Given such a condition, ministers and others have often responded by saying, "You silly people! You ought to believe more. Forget all your questions. Take it on faith. Leap into the dark. Take the initiative. Follow the four easy steps to salvation. Get out there and be born again!" As a pastor, I suppose I have said things like that. Yet today's story reminds us that Christian faith is never so simple as that.

For one thing, Nicodemus *is* taking the initiative. He comes to Jesus as an act of faith. He is drawn from the dark to meet the One who is the Light of the world. Yet when he gets there, this Light casts a shadow on his life. The deeper the conversation gets, the more resistant old Nicodemus becomes.

Have you ever noticed how that is? Sometimes we really want to believe that God reigns over all of human life, that God's love embraces everybody, that God's kingdom comes on earth as it is in heaven. Then we discover what that would mean, and the implications scare us to death.

Say, for instance, like Nicodemus we take the initiative. Suppose we come to ask the central question of the Gospel of John, namely, "Jesus, what is God like?" As we've heard today, the Lord replies, "God gives eternal life to everyone who believes in the Son" (John 3:16).

"Wow!" we reply. "That's good news. I've got eternal life; you've got eternal life. Thank you, Lord, we have all received eternal life."

Jesus clears his throat and says, "I mean, to *everyone* who believes."

"Wait a minute, Lord. What about the murderers in Bosnia, and the cult hero in Switzerland, and the mad bombers in Oklahoma City? What if the Wind should blow on them, and they suddenly believe?"

To which Jesus responds, "Then it's eternal life for them, too." The implications are frightening.

As the Gospel of John puts it, "This is the fundamental crisis of the world: that the light has come into the world, and people loved darkness rather than the light" (3:19). What does that mean? It means that, like Nicodemus, if we take the initiative, if we move closer to Jesus, if we move closer toward the Light, the longer our doubting shadows may fall.

For another thing, when all is said and done, the life Jesus comes to bring, the life of the Eternal One, finally does not depend on our initiative. The life of Christ within us does not depend on the quality of our faltering faith, but on the wild, mysterious grace of God. For Jesus said, "Nicodemus, you must be born anew."

"How can that be?" Nicodemus replied. "I'm an old man, as old as Father Abraham."

Jesus insisted, "Nicodemus, you must be born again."

The confused Pharisee said, "How can that be? Can somebody enter Mommy's womb a second time?"

"Nicodemus," Jesus clarified, "you must be born from above."

Still in the dark, we might imagine old Nick retorting, "How can that be? I never asked to be born in the first place."

Jesus responded by saying, in effect, "Birth is a gift. Eternal life is a gift. Your ability to see the kingdom of God, why, that's a gift! That is to say, faith is a gift, a new kind of birth from the womb of our Mother who art in heaven. So it is, with everyone who is born of the Spirit."

In his striving for faith, Nicodemus wants to know how this can be. He is grabbing for what can only be received as a gift of grace. The good news is that all of his questions, all of his doubts, all of his pursuits of faith, are caught up in the Wind, covered by the sound of a fierce, holy breeze howling in the dark.

"At the age of sixteen," writes Alec Guinness, "I arose from under the hands of the Bishop of Lewes a confirmed atheist." At the age of 41, Guinness returned to the church. He does not have much to say about the years in between. Once in a while he read a religious book, or visited a worship service, or spent the weekend in a monastery. Other than that he saw merely a few glimpses of light in the midst of darkness. Then one day he went back to the church as a quiet believer, 41 years old and wet from the womb.

Of that return, he writes: "There had been no emotional upheaval, no great insight, certainly no proper grasp of theological issues; just a sense of history and the fittingness of things. Something impossible to explain. Teilhard de Chardin says, 'The incommunicable part of us is the pasture of God.' I must leave it at that."[3]

Out in a dark world, if you listen, you can hear the Wind of God's Spirit groaning with the sound of grace, blowing wild and free. If you look, really look, sometimes you'll notice that wherever the Spirit blows, one by one, God's would-be believers are brought to life.

1. Alec Guinness, *Blessings in Disguise* (New York: Warner Books, 1985), p. 23.

2. William Muehl, *Why Preach? Why Listen?* (Philadelphia: Fortress Press, 1986), p. 11.

3. Guinness, pp. 42-43.

Sent From
The Mountain

There is nothing like taking part in a worship service with 17,000 people. If you are surrounded by a choir that large, all of the hymns sound in tune. With that many people gathered to pray in the same place at the same time, you have no doubt God will hear somebody in the crowd. And when a super-charged speaker stands up to challenge people to follow the commandments of Christ, the group dynamics of such a huge crowd ensure that someone, somewhere, is ready to answer the challenge.

That was the case in December 1979, at a mission conference in Urbana, Illinois. Mobs of college students descended upon the campus of the University of Illinois during Christmas break. They came in chartered buses and Volkswagen vans. Every morning was filled with Bible study, prayer, and singing. Each night featured inspirational speeches about what God was doing in our world. And every afternoon, there were opportunities to meet church workers from many different countries. The whole Urbana experience challenged Christian college students to go out into the world and make disciples of all nations.

On the final night of the convention, a famous evangelist stood to speak. He had been informed that he was preaching to the converted, a fact that he took with a grain of salt. Maybe that's why he couldn't help but invite us to stand to prove we were

Christians. After that, he invited all who were standing to consider serving as missionaries. "Will you follow Jesus Christ anywhere?" he asked. "Yes!" came the roar of the crowd.

"Will you do anything he wants you to do?" A second time, the crowd roared, "Yes!"

"Will you go anywhere he asks?" Again the crowd roared, "Yes!"

"If that's true," he said, "then I want you all to obey the Great Commission of Jesus Christ. Go into all nations and seek out the unbelievers. Go and tell them that they're going to perish without Jesus. The time is short. Go into the world and serve God as missionaries."

As I remember back, that five-day convention was a mountain-top experience in my life. It happened at a time when I felt the first stirring of a call to ministry. The pastor of my church had sensed my interest, and encouraged me to go to the convention. I returned home exhausted from the trip and enlivened by the emotional experience. I tried to explain to my very patient parents that I was thinking about becoming a missionary. I was going to go out and conquer the world for Christ. By a week later, however, my enthusiasm had faded. The convention was a memory. There was no huge choir to support my feeble voice, no emotional props to boost my morale, and no baritone preacher telling me what I should do with my life. As I look back on that moment of lost enthusiasm, I now realize how deeply I misunderstood the Great Commission.

The church has often turned to these final words in the Gospel of Matthew to bolster the missionary effort. Jesus sends his followers "to the nations." That's a striking change, since he has spent most of his time tending only to the lost sheep of Israel (Matthew 15:24). But the Great Commission was given on Easter day. The risen Christ gathered his disciples together with the authority of his resurrection, and then he sent them into the world.

Ever since, the church has assumed that *we have* something the world doesn't have. We have a Word to speak, a message to proclaim, a story to tell to the nations. In the late 1700s, a man named Samson Occum was ordained as a Presbyterian minister.

He was Native American, and he was sent as a missionary to the Oneida Indians. On the day of his ordination and commissioning, the preacher based his sermon on the Great Commission.[1] The point was clear: "White people like us have given an Indian like you something you did not have, and we want you to give it away to as many Indian people as you can."

In the late 1700s, that may or may not have been a good idea. History tells many sad stories of European Christians who spoke to people who were neither European nor Christian. They tried to make these people Christians, but inevitably tainted them as Europeans. Frequently it was conversion by coercion. Let's confess, some people were better off before the Christian missionaries got to them. Progress and firepower have not been universally positive influences among innocent civilizations.

These days, it is even more difficult for thoughtful Christians to play the old missionary game of "we've got it and you need it." For one thing, we can no longer assume that people of other cultures haven't heard the gospel. There are untouched areas of the globe, to be sure. But in most cases, the good news has been published, broadcast, and spoken in hundreds of tongues. For another thing, we cannot affirm that we have whatever we think others do not have. People of all nations may have heard the gospel of Jesus Christ and ignored it. The question is: have those of us in this nation done much better? Do we really bear the very News that we so proudly want to give to the nations? That is the challenge of our commission.

Some years ago, novelist Walker Percy spoke to a group of graduating seniors at a Catholic college. He saluted their dedication to study. In glowing terms, he affirmed their call to spread the gospel to people around the world. Yet he couldn't help but note the difficulty of the task. At one point, Percy looked them in the eye and said,

> *Here, surely, is the most difficult challenge of all: to proclaim the Good News in a world whose values seem increasingly indifferent to the very meaning of the Good News. It is a strange world indeed, a world which is, on*

41

*the one hand, more eroticized than ancient Rome, and
yet a world in which the Good News is proclaimed more
loudly and frequently than ever before by TV evangelists
and the new fundamentalists. There occurs a kind of
devaluation of language, a cheapening of the very
vocabulary of salvation, as a consequence of which the
ever-fresh, ever-joyful meaning of the Gospel comes
across as the dreariest TV commercial. How to proclaim
the Good News in a society which never needed it more
but in which language itself has been subverted. Salvation
comes by hearing, according to Scripture, but what is
the hearer of the Good News to do when the hearing
becomes as overloaded as the circuits on an $89 TV set?*[2]

We live in an age where the gospel has been proclaimed on
bumper stickers in every industrialized nation. The strange irony
is that it hasn't seemed to do much good. Perhaps the reason has
little to do with the good news, and everything to do with the
messengers. "Go and make disciples," Jesus said. But we cannot
do that unless we ourselves are committed disciples. "Go and teach
people all that I have commanded you," says the Teacher of the
Sermon on the Mount. We cannot do that if our only study of the
Bible is a little bit of verse-surfing before breakfast to keep us
healthy, wealthy, and wise. Any church that takes the Great
Commission seriously must move into deeper waters, and not
merely throw a wider net into the shallows.

It is striking that Matthew seems to know this. He begins this
triumphant story of Easter with a pathetic note. "The eleven
disciples went to Galilee." That's an incomplete church, as you
know. Once there were twelve disciples. No thanks to Judas, the
church shrank from twelve to eleven. "And when they saw Jesus,
they worshiped him; but some doubted." Even on Easter, with the
risen Lord in plain view, the incomplete church has an incomplete
faith. This is the kind of church that Jesus sends out from the
mountain-top. It's a church that can no longer play, "We've got it
and you need it." The only thing we can say is, "*All of us need it.*"
All of us need a Word that sets us free and sends us forth. Blessed

are those who are poor enough in spirit to receive and obey a crucified Savior.

There is a powerful scene in the movie *The Mission.* Mendoza, a man of the sword, has killed his brother in a fit of anger. No one is surprised. Mendoza is well-known throughout colonial South America as a brutal slave trader who captures the natives and sells them to the Spaniards. But he is overcome by unexpected remorse at the death. He goes into seclusion. A Jesuit priest visits him and suggests a penance to purge his torment. The penance is to join the priest and other Jesuit missionaries as they return to the jungle to work among the natives. Mendoza agrees. They set out on their journey. Mendoza binds up his armor in a huge net. He ties this huge burden to his back and drags it along as a reminder of his violent life. It slows down the travelers, but they continue on.

At one point, the missionaries climb to the top of a great waterfall. Their friends among the natives have been anxiously waiting for their return. The two groups hug one another and shout for joy. Then a native spots Mendoza struggling behind with his bundle of armor. Recognizing him, he grabs a knife, runs to the weary slave trader, and poises to slit his throat in revenge. Mendoza prepares himself for certain death. What he doesn't count on is that the natives have begun to learn a new way from the Jesuits, whereby no one repays evil for evil, enemies are loved, and persecutors are prayed for. The native flashes the knife, then cuts away Mendoza's bundle of armor. His burden of violence falls away and dashes to the bottom of the waterfall. Now free for the first time in years, Mendoza cries like a baby fresh from the womb of God. Soon the priest says, "Welcome home, brother." Then his instruction begins.

Jesus commissions his church both to *be disciples* and to *make disciples.* Disciples are people who have the capacity to cut others free from their burdens, who act out of mercy rather than retaliation, who welcome fellow travelers home from their journeys. Simple converts will not do. "Discipleship," someone notes, "means the engagement of the whole life in following Jesus on the way of the kingdom."[3] Jesus trained his disciples not only to believe the right doctrine, but also to live and die in the right way. He commended

Peter for believing that he is "the Messiah, the Son of the living God" (Matthew 16:16). Yet he also rebuked Peter for denying the way of self-denial and the cross (Matthew 16:21-26). Disciples are formed, not merely informed. Jesus commissions us to teach the gospel, and to do so in a way that creates the kind of people who understand the gospel's claims and live as if those claims are true.

The place to begin is on the mountain, the same "mountain to which Jesus had directed them." The church has stood with Jesus on that mountain before. The devil once took Jesus to a very high mountain and showed him all the world's kingdoms and their splendor. Then the tempter said, "All these I will give to you, if you will fall down and worship me" (Matthew 4:8-9). But rather than accept the splendor, Jesus took up the cross. And only the Christ who gave his life in sacrifice can say, "All authority in heaven and earth has been given to me."

The place to mature is on the mountain, the same mountain where the church has stood with Jesus before. That was the day Jesus took Peter, James, and John, and led them up a high mountain. He was transfigured before them, his face shone like the sun, and the Eternal Word began to talk with Moses the lawgiver and Elijah the prophet. Peter stammered out, "Lord, this is a Kodak moment; can't we capture it and institutionalize it somehow?" Suddenly a bright cloud overshadowed them on the mountain, and a voice said, "This is my Beloved Son; with him I am well pleased" (Matthew 17:1-6). That day the promise of Christmas was confirmed; this Jesus is Emmanuel, God-with-us always, even to the end of the age.

The place to grow up as disciples is on the mountain. Matthew says we have been on the mountain before with Jesus. For Jesus went up the mountain, gathered us together, sat down, and began to teach, saying, "Blessed are the poor in spirit, for theirs is the kingdom of heaven. You are the salt of the earth. Love your enemies. Be complete as your heavenly Father is complete. Do not store up treasures on earth. Seek first the kingdom of God. Enter through the narrow gate. The good person brings good things out of a good treasure. Whoever gives a cup of cold water to these little ones will not lose their reward. Humble yourself like a little child. Pick up your cross and follow me. Forgive one another seventy times seven. Just as you did it to the least of these, you did it to me." We have been on the mountain to sit as those who are taught. The Risen Lord calls us to obey every teaching he has commanded us.

Lesslie Newbigin once noted that every organization or entity can be defined either by its boundaries or its center. The church, he notes, is sent to every nation, so it can never be bounded by local limits or national interests. But the church *is* defined by its center. As he puts it,

> *It is impossible to define exactly the boundaries of the church, and the attempt to do so always ends in an unevangelical legalism. But it is always possible and necessary to define the centre. The church is its proper self, and is a sign of the kingdom, only insofar as it continually points men and women beyond itself to Jesus and invites them to conversion and commitment to him.*[4]

Sisters and brothers, we have a Word to speak, a message to proclaim, and a story to tell the nations. Jesus Christ is risen, with authority from beyond heaven and earth. He has claimed us with the love and justice of a Holy God. Jesus promises to be present with us, always meddling in our lives, until we become the kind of people who share God's justice and love with every person under heaven.

That, if you ask me, is the meaning, and the promise, of the Great Commission.

---

1. James H. Smylie, Dean K. Thompson, and Cary Patrick, *Go Therefore: 150 Years of Presbyterians in Global Mission*, ed. Cary Patrick (Atlanta: Presbyterian Publishing House, 1987), p. v.

2. Walker Percy, "A Cranky Novelist Reflects on the Church,"*Signposts in a Strange Land* (New York: Farrar, Straus, and Giroux, 1991), p. 322.

3. Mortimer Arias, "Rethinking the Great Commission," *Theology Today* 47/4 (January 1991), p. 412.

4. Lesslie Newbigin, *Sign of the Kingdom* (Grand Rapids: William B. Eerdmans Publishing Co., 1980), p. 68.

A Taste
Of Life

The workshop was winding up. About 25 pleasant church people had gathered in central Pennsylvania to take part in a workshop on worship. The better part of a Saturday morning had dealt with a variety of topics, such as the order of worship, the role of music, the place of preaching, and whether or not children should come to the Lord's table. A few stomachs were growling for lunch when I asked, "Does anybody have any questions?" Most people smiled and sat in that circle of metal folding chairs. One woman, however, thought for a minute and then shot up her hand. She said, "You know, there's something I've always wondered about. Why do we bother with Maundy Thursday?"

The question came out of the blue; it was some time in October, and no time close to Holy Week. I said, "I'm not sure what you are asking."

She clarified the question. "Christians are Easter People. We celebrate the resurrection of Jesus Christ. So why do we observe Maundy Thursday?"

I asked, "Do you have a problem with the death of Jesus? Or do you have concerns about the trial and crucifixion and all of that?"

"No," she said, "Good Friday is essential to the story. You can't celebrate the resurrection if nobody died. Jesus died; and his death holds great significance. No, what I want to know is why most

47

churches have a worship service on Maundy Thursday. It is such a dark and gloomy night, with all of that talk about thirty pieces of silver, the garden of Gethsemane, and Peter's denial. I know the story is in the Bible, but I don't think we need to honor it with a worship service. Why not remember the cross on Good Friday and the resurrection on Easter? Isn't that enough?"

Fortunately, time ran out before I could finish mumbling my half-baked answer. It was obvious from the confused glances and wilted handshakes that the question had dampened the genial enthusiasm of the group. Most folks present could have handled questions on the mechanics of worship, such as, "Should ushers wear sneakers?" or "How do you introduce unfamiliar hymns to the congregation?" But this person was questioning the purpose of observing a well-established church holy day. As she put it, "Why do we bother with Maundy Thursday?"

Given some time to think about it, we could come up with a number of answers. As the writer of Mark tells the story, the day we call Maundy Thursday was the last occasion that Jesus spent an evening with his disciples. The events surrounding that night became the acid test of true discipleship. Jesus ate a Passover meal with the twelve disciples, announcing that someone within that inner circle would betray him. After singing a hymn, the whole group went to the Mount of Olives, where Jesus warned that all of them would desert him. As he prayed in Gethsemane, his closest companions fell asleep. Then, while Jesus was still chastising the sleepy disciples, Judas appeared with a gang of thugs, and betrayed the Lord with a kiss. With that, says Mark, "all of them deserted him and fled" (Mark 14:50).

For many Christians, the age-old inference has been that if you can watch, wait, and stay faithful on a night like Maundy Thursday, then you must truly belong to the inner circle of Jesus' followers. If you can survive the telling of Mark 14, then you may be worthy to remain within the fellowship of the church.

Unfortunately, that has not always had the desired effect of producing committed believers. A middle-aged woman tells how she first joined a Lutheran church as a teenager on Maundy Thursday. "I had to sit through a lot of boring classes with our minister," she said. "After enduring weeks of strict instruction, we approached the night of our membership reception. We wore dark clothing and sat in the front pew. The minister preached a sermon about how horrible it would be for us to betray Jesus. Then he called us forward, and we joined the church. It was a gloomy conclusion to a dreary class. Not coincidentally, it was the last time I sat in a church for a number of years."

"Why bother with Maundy Thursday?" Others claim that Maundy Thursday, like no other occasion, is drenched with a mood which lies at the heart of true Christian discipleship. And if we cannot watch and wait and feel a little bit guilty, then we don't know what it means to follow Jesus Christ. That is, the story of Jesus' final evening with his disciples is intended to evoke a recognition of our sinfulness. "Truly I tell you," the Lord says, "one of you will betray me, one who is eating with me" (Mark 14:18). Those who hear him begin to exchange glances and say, "Surely, you're not talking about me, are you?"

For such people, Christian piety means beating your breast and wallowing in perpetual self-examination. Faith is incomplete until they can sing the words of a favorite hymn,

> *Who was the guilty? Who brought this upon you?*
> *It is my treason, Lord, that has undone You.*
> *'Twas I, Lord Jesus, I it was denied You;*
> *I crucified You.*[1]

A minister friend once told me about the biting criticism he received from an austere member of his congregation. The member said, "Reverend, the problem with you is that every Sunday you stand up and tell me that I am forgiven. Obviously you don't know how evil I am, otherwise you wouldn't forgive me so much." When my colleague expressed a bold word about how we are justified with God by grace through faith, the man replied, "You don't understand, Reverend. I come to church so I can feel guilty about my sins." Perhaps the man wishes every day was Maundy Thursday.

I believe we need to affirm what the woman at that workshop said. We are God's Easter people. We are gathered, not by a single sinister episode from the story of Jesus, but by a complete narrative of sin and forgiveness, death and resurrection. This story is fleshed out in the final meal that Jesus ate with his disciples. The scriptures tell us Jesus instituted two important practices around that table. First, he washed his disciples' feet and said, "I want all of you to wash each other's feet" (John 13:14). That, of course, is a practice which most Protestants would never go for, although it has always set the example for Christian service.

The other thing Jesus did was to take bread, and bless it, and break it, and *give* it to his disciples. From the beginning, the followers of Jesus have received these gifts around the table of the Lord. The bread and wine are not given to test our faithfulness. They are not intended to toss believers into a murky pool of guilt. The loaf and the cup are given, and received, as gifts. Through these gifts, our relationship with Christ is nourished, sustained, and increased.[2] Our only appropriate response to such generosity is to offer a word of thanks.

Taken without a sense of gratitude, the story we heard from the Gospel of Mark becomes subject to an unduly sorrowful interpretation. It is the story of the Last Supper, the final occasion for Jesus to be with his disciples. Already we know that Judas has cut a deal with the chief priests. He will turn over Jesus for a handful of coins. This is the last time Jesus will eat with his closest friends. The shadow of gloom is so heavy that you can cut it with a knife.

Historically this grim, thankless mood has been perpetuated as some Christians gather at the table for communion. A sour-faced minister in black intones the words, "This is the joyful feast of the people of God," never sensing the irony of what is said. Chunks of bread are distributed by people with the countenance of pallbearers. As the bread and wine are served, organ music in a minor key reminds the recipients they are not worthy to receive this supernatural gift. The message is clear: "This is the Last Supper, observed under the shadow of darkness, betrayal, and death."

If I may speak my mind, however, the church has no right to observe the Last Supper. Instead it is our duty and delight to observe the Lord's Supper. There is profound difference between Last Supper and Lord's Supper. The Last Supper took place on the eve of Jesus' departure, a night filled with anguish, abandonment, and loss. What Christians celebrate is the Lord's Supper, the feast of the Risen Lord. We cannot come to this table and pretend Easter has not happened. Christ is risen; and that reality is the means by which any of us can come to this table. We come not merely in repentance, but in gratitude. God has raised up Jesus; and that is the only reason to gather for worship on this day, or any other day. We come, not to mourn the dearly departed Lord, but to receive the gift of his life.

For isn't that what he says? "Take; this is my body." Or to paraphrase it, "This is the essence of my life, and I put it into your hands. I give my life to all of you as I gave up my life for all of you." Then he adds, "This is my blood of the covenant, which is poured out for many." According to Mark, Jesus gives his blood to pay the ransom (Mark 10:45), to purchase us back from the forces in the world that would hurt and destroy. Jesus gives his blood to establish a relationship with all of us, that we would know we belong to him. "I give you my life; I claim you as my own."

Christian faith is nourished through receiving and responding to this gift. As John Calvin wrote in one of his letters, "The moment we receive Christ by faith as he offers himself in the gospel, we become truly members of his body, and life flows into us from him as from the head. For by no other way does he reconcile us to God by the sacrifice of his death than because he is ours and we are one with him . . . Thus we draw life from his flesh and blood, so that they are not undeservedly called our 'food.' "[3]

If we come to a Maundy Thursday table as God's Easter people, suddenly the whole occasion comes into focus. Jesus gives himself to us and for us. As we participate, we remember the story of our redemption. We claim the strength to abide in the thick of suffering. If we should watch our small corner of the world descend into horror, we can trust that horror will not speak the last word. We remember that we belong to Jesus, even when we are tempted to turn away from him. And we wait for the day, the final day, when suffering, horror, and temptation will pass away . . . when we shall eat and drink in the fullness of God's kingdom.

51

These are some of the reasons why we bother with Maundy Thursday. The table set before us tempers the Easter life with the reality of the cross. Even in the assurance of the resurrection, we cannot be glib or naive. The gifts of this supper are given in the midst of suffering. They are signs of grace, signals of love, pieces of evidence that God will continue what God alone has started. They are promises of Christ's life, given to us in the midst of a world of suffering and death.

Maybe that's why we often take such a little piece of bread and sip a tiny cup. We have only a taste of what it means to belong to Christ. It is never the whole experience, but simply a taste. And a taste of life is enough to sustain us.

In 1984, novelist Reynolds Price discovered he had a malignant tumor in his spine. There came a point in his illness when he felt the need to reconnect with his Methodist roots. Since he was staying with a cousin at the time, he asked her to contact her minister and request the sacrament of communion.

The minister arrived on a hot morning. Price sat alone in a chair in his bedroom. He listened as the pastor read the words of institution from the Gospel of Mark — "This is my body, this is my blood, do this in memory of me." Then he ate the bread and drank the cup. Of that occasion, Price writes,

> *Perhaps as intensely as any mystic, in the slow eating that one morning, I experienced again the almost overwhelming force which has always felt to me like God's presence. Whether the force would confirm my healing or go on devastating me, for the moment I barely cared. No prior taste in my old life had meant as much as this new chance at a washed and clarified view of my fate — and that from the hands of a strange young minister in a room which didn't belong to me.*[4]

It was only a taste, with meager portions of bread and wine. The sacrament did not mend his body. Neither did it set him free from weakness and confinement. But it did give him a taste of Christ's presence. And that taste was sufficient to sustain his appetite.

52

1. Johann Heerman, "Ah, Holy Jesus," *The Presbyterian Hymnal* (Louisville: Westminster/John Knox Press, 1990), p. 93.

2. B. A. Gerrish, *Grace and Gratitude: The Eucharistic Theology of John Calvin* (Minneapolis: Fortress Press, 1993), p. 134.

3. As quoted in Gerrish, *Grace and Gratitude,* p. 128.

4. Reynolds Price, *A Whole New Life: An Illness and A Healing* (New York: Penguin Books, 1995), p. 81.

Mark 2:23—3:6 (C, RC) Proper 4
Mark 2:23-28 (L) Pentecost 2
Ordinary Time 9

Can
Christians Dance?

A few years ago, I was asked to serve as the worship leader at a regional church conference for teenagers. The enthusiastic recruiter told me about the wonderful experience I could expect from the gathering. "Every summer," she said, "the conference brings together about a hundred or so young people at a camp that has no swimming pool. We gather during the dog days of August. The conference is so much fun, nobody misses the pool!"

My assignment was to preach sermons, lead some singing, and pray. Upon my arrival, however, I was given a second job by the camp director. She had a smirk on her face as she reminded me of the developmental characteristics of late adolescents. Then, with a twinkle in her eye, she said, "It is the worship leader's job to preserve the high moral standards of the camp." That explains why, about midnight each night, I was handed a high intensity flashlight, pointed to the bushes, and instructed to search for teenagers whose hormones were working overtime. The camp staff called it "Smut Patrol."

On Tuesday night at curfew time, I began to make my rounds. I had dressed in black clothing and carried my trusty Ray-O-Vac flashlight. Fortunately it was a quiet night. It was early in the week and few romances had begun to bloom. Suddenly I heard loud rock and roll music. Coming around the edge of a meadow, a dreadful sight came into view. About a hundred teenagers had gathered beneath a picnic pavilion. They were moving to the rhythms of the music. "My God," I thought, "this is church camp! What would John Calvin think?"

The camp director had been clear. My job was to preserve decency and order. Running to the pavilion. I climbed up a picnic table and shouted, "Wait! It's curfew! It's the wrong time to dance." But the music kept playing. The teenagers kept dancing. Much to my shock, one of them moved toward me, her arm outstretched, inviting me to move to the rhythms of the night. I didn't know what to do. Should I stick to my guns, and unplug the music? Or should I join in a dance which broke all the rules?

It was not a new dilemma. In fact, this issue lies at the heart of these two stories from Mark. Some people in the time of Jesus struggled with the same problem. They probably did not dress in black. They did not carry spotlights. They certainly did not consider themselves Presbyterians. But they were gravely concerned about keeping the rules.

One day, they saw Jesus and his disciples waltzing in the fields. Apparently Jesus gave his friends permission to pluck and eat the grain. Now, what did the rules say about that? On the one hand, it is always proper that the hungry be fed. The book of Deuteronomy says if someone is hungry and traveling through a neighbor's field, it is legal to take your neighbor's excess food. That's what neighbors are for: to keep one another well-fed (Deuteronomy 23:25).

On the other hand, that particular day was the Sabbath. And everybody knew the rules concerning the Holy Day of God. "Six days you shall labor and do all your work. But the seventh day is a Sabbath to the LORD your God; you shall not do any work — you, or your son or your daughter, or your male or female slave, or your ox or your donkey, or any of your livestock, or the resident alien in your towns" (Deuteronomy 5:13-14).

So the Rule Keepers questioned Jesus, "Why are you letting your followers break the rules?"

Jesus said, "There is a precedent for this. Haven't you read about King David in the Bible?" Of course, they read the Bible. The Bible was the Rule Book, after all. It was full of statutes for every sticky situation. This Galilean upstart was disrupting a time-honored tradition, and justifying it with a minor footnote to a wayward king. And if that jab wasn't annoying enough, they heard Jesus ask them, "Would you like to dance?" The Rule Keepers glared at him.

They kept watching as Jesus danced into the sanctuary of worship. There was a person in that place with a crinkled-up hand. Nobody doubted Jesus had power to heal him. But it presented a tougher situation. In the Bible, there are no obvious rules about healing crinkled-up hands. So what should be done? It is true that human need demands a compassionate response. But it is also true that the worship of God should never get "out of hand." The assembly of the faithful should be a holy and pious occasion; isn't that right? Most people have learned the three rules about worship, namely, "Sit up, shut up, and pay up." But along came Jesus, ready to help a crinkled-up man do the fox-trot. It broke all the rules anyone cared to remember.

Which is more lawful: to tend to someone in need, or to keep the Sabbath rules? Which is more expedient: to save someone's withered life, or to squelch a troublemaker? As Jesus made his decision to heal, the Rule Keepers decided to kill. According to the Gospel of Mark, they said, "It's time to stop Jesus from dancing." They plotted his assassination, and they were successful. They unplugged the music. As a familiar hymn speaks for Jesus,

> *I danced on the Sabbath and I cured the lame;*
> *The holy people said it was a shame.*
> *They whipped and they stripped and they hung Me high,*
> *And left Me there on a cross to die.*[1]
> (Sydney Carter. ©1963 by Stainer & Bell Ltd. Used by permission of Hope Publishing Co., Carol Stream, IL 60188. All rights reserved. Used by permission.)

Scholars have observed that the conflict between Jesus and these Pharisees lies close to the heart of Mark's Gospel. It reflects a cosmic battle that began as the Strong One of God announced the gracious reign of God. The forces of evil and oppression can only respond with the language of destruction, saying, "What have you to do with us, Jesus of Nazareth? Have you come to destroy us?" (Mark 1:24). Someone notes, "Jesus' actions are so opposed to what the authorities accept as God's laws that they conclude Jesus could not be acting on God's authority."[2] Therefore, presuming *they* were acting on God's behalf, "The Pharisees went out and immediately conspired with the Herodians against him, how to destroy him" (Mark 3:6).

What these Rule Keepers did not know, however, is that Jesus learned his dance steps from the Lord Almighty, the giver of every good and perfect rule. What the Rule Keepers also did not know is that God never allows his music to be unplugged for longer than three days. They destroyed Jesus, but the stone was rolled away. The tomb was found empty. Ever since, Jesus has danced a Resurrection Two-Step, inviting us to join in the dance as we are able. The hymn continues,

> *They cut me down and I leapt up high;*
> *I am the life that will never, never die;*
> *I'll live in you if you live in Me:*
> *I am the Lord of the Dance, said He.*
>
> *Dance, then, wherever you may be;*
> *I am the Lord of the Dance, said He,*
> *And I'll lead you all, wherever you may be,*
> *And I'll lead you all in the dance, said He.*[3]
> (Sydney Carter. ©1963 by Stainer & Bell Ltd. Used by permission of Hope Publishing Co., Carol Stream, IL 60188. All rights reserved. Used by permission.)

There is a scene in the popular children's book, *The Lion, the Witch, and the Wardrobe,* where the evil White Witch discovers that her power is slipping. The beloved land of Narnia has been under the deadly grip of a perpetual winter. Yet as Aslan the Lion comes to Narnia, the snow begins to thaw. Suddenly the grass turns green, the sky becomes azure blue, and primroses blossom.

"This is no thaw," said the Dwarf to the Witch. "This is *spring.* What are we to do? Your winter has been destroyed, I tell you! This is Aslan's doing." The Witch can only respond with venomous threats. But the coming of the Christ-figure Aslan signifies that a

58

whole new creation is at hand. The good news prompts another, more joyful response.[4]

According to the writer of Mark, this is the essence and invitation of the Gospel. God has begun a new age by sending Jesus Christ into our world. The dance continues, when deserts rejoice and dead flowers blossom. The music swells, as steel hearts are broken open and hardened ears begin to listen.[5] The rhythm invites us to get in step with God's activity in our world, regardless of our preconceived notions and legislated limitations. The music of Resurrection demands a response. It also makes a response possible.

When Rhoda went to the nursing home, nobody ever thought she would walk again, much less dance. She spent her days watching game shows and soap operas, an endless cycle of *Jeopardy* and *General Hospital*. She could hardly move down the hall to the television. When she got there, she could barely see the screen. Everyone thought her days were numbered.

One day the activity director announced, "Rhoda, we're going on a bus trip."

Rhoda said, "I don't want to miss my television shows."

The activity director said, "Don't worry. We'll be back in plenty of time." She was lying, but it got Rhoda on the bus. Rhoda allowed herself to be carried aboard. They put her walker by her side, although nobody thought she would use it.

Soon the bus carried Rhoda to a huge arts and music festival in a nearby city. Attendance at the festival that day numbered over 100,000 people. It was an ambitious task to take 25 nursing home residents to a place like that. It was also a nerve-wracking experience, when the activities director counted 24 heads at the end of the day. Rhoda was missing. They looked high and low. They couldn't find her. In time, they located her aluminum walker near a bandstand in a circus tent, but not Rhoda.

Suddenly someone spotted her. Thirty feet away, she was dancing with a man half her age. "Rhoda," shouted the director, "what are you doing?"

Rhoda said, "It's the polka!"

"But what about your legs?"

Rhoda shouted back, "When I heard the music, I couldn't stop my toes from tapping."

Wasn't that something? She was so caught up in the dance, the life-giving dance, that she forgot the rules which hemmed her in. It was a glimpse, perhaps, of what God requires of us.

So there I was at summer camp, shrouded in black, mouth agape, wondering what I should do. This is the truth: there was no time to think about it. Someone moved toward me with an outstretched arm. Then she grabbed my hand and yanked me into the circle. A curious thing began to happen. My toes began to tap. My knees began to bend. My feet began to bounce. I couldn't help myself. The music swirled around us like a powerful whirlpool, swallowing us up in its wake.

Come to think of it, as I first looked around the edges of that pavilion, I noticed some of you had gone there with me. Let's see: you were there . . . and you . . . and you. Yes, I am sure of it. There we were, standing for a minute as wallflowers around the edges of the life-giving dance. So why did we go to that makeshift dance floor? Did we go to move to the rhythms of the night? Or did we go in a futile attempt to unplug the music?

Whatever the case, the daring dance of Jesus and his kingdom continues, with us or without us. So which shall it be?[6]

1. Sydney Carter, "I Danced in the Morning," *The Presbyterian Hymnal* (Louisville: Westminster/John Knox Press, 1990), p. 302.

2. David Rhoads and Donald Michie, *Mark as Story: An Introduction to the Narrative of a Gospel* (Philadelphia: Fortress Press, 1982), p. 81.

3. Carter, *ibid.*

4. C. S. Lewis, *The Lion, the Witch, and the Wardrobe* (New York: Collier Books, 1970), p. 118.

5. In many ways, the Gospel of Mark may be an exegesis of Isaiah 35:1-10, a new "homecoming" that is manifest in Jesus Christ. Note, for instance, that in the presence of Jesus, even the desert turns "green" (Mark 6:39).

6. For an assessment of this sermon as it was preached in its initial setting, see my article, "The Sermon That Flew," *Journal for Preachers* 16.3 (Easter 1993), pp. 34-36.

Looking A
Little Bit Crazy

A photocopied sign was posted inside a church office. It was one of those humorous full-page slogans that people in different offices duplicate and pass among themselves. Most of us have seen this particular message, I suppose, but posted in a church office, the words took on a new meaning. There it was, taped to the cinder blocks behind a secretary's desk. The sign read, "You don't have to be crazy to work here, but it helps."

At one level, why not put a sign like that in a church? Many churches are busy, hectic, confusing places. There are worship services to plan, educational programs to run, choirs to rehearse, fellowship dinners to organize, and outreach efforts to facilitate. There is a lot going on, and things can get frantic. The running joke in one church I know is that the staff keeps saying, "Next week it's going to get quiet," but the quiet week never comes. The work load can become a little bit crazy.

On a deeper level, there is a great deal of truth to that sign. There is something strange about the church. We are not just another club or civic organization. The church's view of reality is increasingly out of phase from a lot of prevailing views. In the church, we do and say things that do not always make sense to people outside of this house. Here we are, gathered on the weekend, sitting on hard pews instead of lawn chairs. People we know are outside, working on their tans or washing their cars, while we gather here, inside, to lift our voices in prayer and song. As a lot of other people are planning a barbecue or sipping a Bloody Mary, we come together on a morning like this to break the bread and drink the cup. To some outsiders, it must look a little bit crazy.

According to the scripture text we heard a few minutes ago, this perception may reveal something of what it means to be the church. Mark tells us about the day when the immediate family of Jesus came to take him away in a straitjacket. The word on the street was that Jesus was "out of his mind." Taken quite literally, people thought he stood "beside himself." They claimed Jesus was possessed. And so, his family came to his house to take Jesus away, because the popular opinion was that he was insane.

That might sound like an odd assessment of his ministry, but it is central to how the gospel of Mark portrays the work of Jesus. From the beginning, Jesus acted . . . well, he acted as if he was *different*. Jesus announced that God's reign had come near. He acted as if his view of the world was different from the world we have taken for granted.

Recall some of the stories Mark tells. One day, Jesus met the town lunatic in Capernaum, and he set the man free from forces beyond his control. Immediately Jesus met a woman bedridden with a fever. The neighbors said, "I'm sorry; there's nothing we can do." But Jesus set the woman free from her sickness. He set her free for service. Then Jesus met someone with a skin disease so ugly that all its victims were quarantined from the temple. Jesus healed that person's disease, and he set that person free from segregation.

According to Mark, Jesus did not accept the world as a place of sickness, sin, and evil. He acted as if God had begun doing something new. Unlike the peasants and beggars of his time, "his eyes lacked the proper cringe, his voice the proper whine, his walk the proper shuffle."[1] Jesus not only announced the nearness of God's kingdom, he acted as if God's reign had actually come. That's why some people said, "He has gone out of his mind."

The evidence still reinforces that appraisal. For every disturbed person whom Jesus healed, there are twenty people who are possessed by forces outside their control. For every headache Jesus ever relieved, there are fifty more bottles of Tylenol sold every minute. For every ugly, isolating disease Jesus ever healed, a hundred more AIDS patients are admitted to the hospital. Listen! There are forces still at work that hurt, cripple, and destroy human life.

Has the world changed? Try telling that to the family and friends of Jaco Pastorius. A former altar boy from Fort Lauderdale, Pastorius emerged during the late 1970s as a bright new star of the jazz music scene. He was a phenomenal bass player, with a keen ear for harmony and an unsurpassed technical ability on his 1962 Fender bass. He joined the well-known jazz group Weather Report and gained instant acclaim for his musicianship.

With the fame, however, came free access to cocaine and alcohol. As Jaco fell into a routine of drug abuse, he began to exhibit increasingly bizarre behavior. His substance abuse aggravated an undiagnosed manic-depressive condition, which, in turn, prompted a tragic decline into psychosis, institutionalization, and self-destruction. The self-acclaimed "world's greatest jazz bassist" lived the final years of his life as a homeless person in New York's Washington Square Park. Pastorius died in September 1987, following a savage beating by a bar bouncer. A mourner sized up his life as "brilliant goods in a damaged package."[2]

There are untold numbers of tragedies that happen due to human weakness. Others occur by malevolent conspiracies against us. Jesus came preaching, "The kingdom of God is at hand!" But the evidence reveals God's kingdom is a disputed sovereignty.

Has the world changed? That's the issue in the story from the third chapter of Mark. Back in the time of Jesus, some of the best theological minds summed up the evidence. They said, "It seems Jesus has great strength and ability. Yet the world hasn't changed. It appears like Jesus has power over the house of evil. But the house of evil has stone walls and an iron-clad gate."

"Jesus may be doing some good things," they added. "But what if Jesus is a trickster? Perhaps the evil powers have sent him to deceive us. What if Jesus is actually evil in disguise? What if he's been sent to get our hopes up before dashing them once again?"

That is, what if this is the same gruesome, dark, demonic world that we have always known?

Admittedly, this is a curious line of thinking, especially for the New Testament. But look at the evidence. If the powers of destruction and death still rule over the world, what conclusion could make more sense?

So here's the question: Has the world changed? Is there anything qualitatively different with the coming of Jesus? I guess we will have to decide for ourselves.

At least, that's how Jesus confronted the issue. When the best minds of his generation accused him of teaming up with the side of evil, Jesus responded in a way that let people decide for themselves. "Think of it this way," he said. "A kingdom divided cannot stand. A house divided cannot stand." So far so good. That makes sense.

"If I'm on the side of evil," Jesus added, "then the house of evil is collapsing, because I would be working against my own house. And if I'm on the side of God, then I would naturally work against the house of evil."

In other words, Jesus said in effect, "Decide what you want about my ministry; decide whether or not you think I am out of my mind. But either way, know this: the end of evil is already in sight. The house of evil has been plundered."

Is that true? That is the question. Has the world changed with the first coming of Jesus? If nothing has changed, then the future is an endless string of oppression, misery, and defeat. But if the reign of God has intruded upon the status quo, then we can act like Jesus. We can do the will of God. We can confront the powers of hell *as if* God rules over heaven and earth. We can act in the face of death *as if* death has already been defeated. We can gather in a place like this, singing praises to a Savior who has already assured us of the world's redemption. We can stand around the baptismal font to claim God's promises for our children. Trusting in the final triumph of God, we can act redemptively even when the world calls us crazy. Maybe that's what we are: crazy cousins with our odd uncle Jesus. When we live as if God's reign has already come, we find ourselves in a strange new family called "church."

In our time, perhaps no one has seen the true social dimension of God's kingdom more clearly than Martin Luther King, Jr. King confronted the evil house of racism with a clear word of gospel justice. His work provoked allegations against his character and threats against his life. Yet he remained faithful to his vision until the day someone shot him. The key, as he said in a number of his speeches, was a certain *maladjustment*.

> *There are certain things within our social order to which I am proud to be maladjusted and to which I call upon all [people] of good will to be maladjusted. If you will allow the preacher in me to come out now, let me say to you that I never did intend to adjust to the evils of segregation and discrimination. I never did intend to adjust myself to religious bigotry. I never did intend to adjust myself to economic conditions that will take necessities from the many to give luxuries to the few. I never did intend to adjust myself to the madness of militarism, and the self-defeating effects of physical violence. And I call upon all [people] of good will to be maladjusted because it may well be that the salvation of the world lies in the hands of the maladjusted.*

So, concluded King, "Let us be as maladjusted as Jesus of Nazareth, who could look into the eyes of the men and women of his generation and cry out, 'Love your enemies. Bless them that curse you. Pray for them that despitefully use you.' "[3]

Has the world changed? Every one of us must decide, just as Dr. King made his decision. We live our lives by the assumptions we make. If we assume Jesus Christ has broken into the violence-prone, death-dealing house of evil, then we must act accordingly.

A friend named Bill is a minister. He also has been accused of being a little bit nuts. Bill does workshops for churches on clowning. Not long ago, he was in a distant city, packing up after a workshop. The phone rang. Nobody was around. He answered. "Are you a minister?" somebody asked.

"Yes, actually I am."

"Come quickly," said the voice, "our child is dying of leukemia."

Bill dropped everything. He ran out to his rental car and drove to the hospital. He parked the car, ran up the steps, through the double doors, and down the hall. Suddenly it hit him: he was still dressed as a clown, with a white face, red nose, orange hair, and green suspenders. He didn't have time to change. It was an emergency. He kept going. He found the room, knocked on the door, and entered the room where a young girl in a hospital bed lay surrounded by her family.

"We called for a minister, not a clown," said the father. The child replied, "He's better than a minister. Can he stay?" No one dared to deny her request. Bill sat on the edge of the hospital bed. He sang songs. He told Bible stories. He cradled the little girl in his arms until the end. When the last moment came, she made a final request. "Would you come to my funeral?"

So that's how it happened. On the third day, crazy Bill stood with white face, red nose, orange hair, and green suspenders. He never spoke a word, yet he led the people as they laughed, and cried, and remembered the little girl's life. A few people present thought it was wrong to have a clown at a funeral, much less lead the service. They murmured afterwards, "That minister is out of his mind! He's crazy!" By all the proper canons of pastoral protocol, they were probably correct.

But there he stood, acting as if God's joyful power has already defeated death. Was he crazy? Who can say? All we know is that Bill heard Jesus say, "I am the resurrection and the life," and he acted accordingly.

"You don't have to be crazy to work around here, but it helps." Likewise, you don't have to be out of your mind to do the work of Jesus Christ, even though a faithful life can provoke the world to think of you that way. Should evil conspire against you, listen closely. You may hear Christ say, "You're my brother — you're my sister — you're my family."

---

1. John Dominic Crossan, *Jesus: A Revolutionary Biography* (New York: HarperCollins, 1994), p. 194.

2. Bill Milkowski, *Jaco: The Extraordinary and Tragic Life of Jaco Pastorius* (San Francisco: Miller Freeman Books, 1995), p. 213.

3. Martin Luther King, Jr., "The American Dream,"*A Testament of Hope: The Essential Writings and Speeches of Martin Luther King, Jr.* (New York: HarperCollins, 1986), p. 216.

How To Plant
An English Garden

A service club gathers for lunch each week in a nearby hotel. After lunch and a little business, someone from the group usually introduces a speaker. Club members rarely know in advance what the program will be. They may hear from a Mexican exchange student, a tax attorney, or a team of skydivers. They discover the topic when they arrive.

Anticipation was high when one speaker arrived with a carousel of slides. Much to the chagrin of many, he was introduced as a landscaper with an interest in English gardens. But as he began to talk, the audience was captivated by his insight and ability. He showed slides of beautiful British gardens, each one a dance of color and vitality. He explained why individual plants are chosen for their size, shape, and color. He spoke about the importance of a careful design for each garden.

Along the way, he made an observation. "There are two ways to plant an English garden," he said. "One way is to mark the garden in careful plots. You plant one kind of perennial here, another over there, a shrub over there. Keep each plot distinct, and then weed the areas in between. That is a high maintenance garden which requires constant work."

"The other way," he said, "is to plant some bulbs in a cluster over here and over there, throw some seeds around in between, and let it happen. Don't worry about the weeding. *Just plant the garden and let it go.*"

Now, that was a novel idea. Have you ever heard of anybody who plants a garden and lets it go? I am neither a farmer nor a specialist in horticulture, but the few gardens I have known were more work than they were worth. I grew up on the northern edge of the Appalachian mountains. After the first spring rain every year, my father would fire up his roto-tiller and break up the soil. It was my job to follow behind, pick up the winter crop of rocks, and throw them off to the side. It was hard work. We had to harvest the rocks before we could plant the vegetables. Each trench was dragged open by a hoe. Onions went here, corn went there, lettuce was planted in a row. When the crops sprouted, my sister and I were sent to weed the garden. I was marginally competent at the task. Once I yanked up a whole row of green beans and threw them on the weed pile. Yet I never thought you could plant a garden and let it go.

Nevertheless, that was what the man said. And that is what Jesus said in one of the parables we have heard. He tells us about someone who planted a garden and left it alone. The sower did not worry about weeding. Neither did he worry about rocks. He just scattered the seed, and let the seed do all the work. Here is a picture of letting go, of someone who relinquishes control, of business without busy-ness. For people like me, it is a picture that is difficult to keep in focus.

Most of us want to think we are indispensable. We wake up each day hoping to fuel the world with our enthusiasm and boundless strength. At Ronald Reagan's inauguration, the President read for us an entry from the diary of Private Martin Treptow. We were ready to hear such energetic words. Private Treptow was an obscure World War I hero. The new President read this entry from his journal: "America must win this war. Therefore I will work, I will save, I will sacrifice, I will endure. I will fight cheerfully and do my utmost as if the issue of the whole struggle depended upon me."

Too bad Mr. Reagan didn't go on. The next entry in the journal reads, "Getting a poor start. 8:30 in the morning, still in bed singing

'Home, Sweet Home.' "[1] We can understand that, can't we? Some mornings we wake in the earnest desire to take the world by storm. When we forget to set the alarm clock, we awake late after the best sleep ever.

In the two parables we hear from Mark, Jesus points to the great potential in things that look passive. A farmer works hard in the field, but having planted a crop he must get on with his life. Each day has a rhythm of eating, drinking, and sleeping. The parable insists that he has to sleep. He wakes up on many days when all he can do is walk out and see that little seems to happen. When the harvest comes, the man lets it come because his life depends upon it. The text assures us this farmer is quick to put in the sickle. But there is a period when all he can do is wait. Just let it happen. It is hard for a lot of us to do that.

Then there is the mustard seed, proverbially the smallest of all. Perhaps there are smaller seeds, like the alfalfa seed and others. But this little mustard seed in the soil explodes into a bush massive enough to shade the birds of the air. No one hovers over the germination and growth; the seed carries its mysterious future in a way hidden from ordinary human observation. Its potential is beyond all speculation.

Left to us, we might want to pursue more aggressive measures. Somebody put up a sign along a stretch of interstate highway. It was a large white slab of plywood with blood-red letters. Planted in a cow pasture, the ominous sign announced, "The kingdom of God is coming at any time; repent and believe the good news. Bible Fellowship Church." The sign painters intended this apocalyptic message to affect the changed lives of every passing traveler. And certainly, many saw the makeshift billboard and stepped on the gas. Everybody, that is, except the cows in that field. They didn't look too upset about God's approaching kingdom. Some cows were chewing. Others were sleeping. Some simply stood there, as only cows can stand in a field.

It looked like something Jesus would say. "Go to the cow and consider her ways." Announce the kingdom and sow the seeds; then grab a bite to eat, take a nap, and stand around in patience. God's coming reign is beyond all calculated human effort. We do what we can, and spend the rest of the time living. Robert Capon points out,

> Once the man in the parable has sown the seed, he does nothing more than mind his own business. He goes to bed at night and gets up in the morning — and then he shops at the supermarket, unclogs the sink, whips up a gourmet supper, plays chamber music with his friends, watches the eleven o-clock news, and goes to bed again. And he does that and nothing but that, day after day after day — while all along the seed that is the kingdom sprouts and grows in a way that he himself simply knows nothing about.[2]

The best lesson may come from a little girl who plants cherry tomato seeds in a paper cup. One day her father helps to fill the cup with topsoil. She pokes a hole in the soil with her finger, drops in the seeds, smooths over the top, and gives the cup to her daddy, who puts the cup on the kitchen windowsill. Then she says, "Is it a tomato yet?" Assured it will take a while, she runs off to play.

A few minutes later, the little girl runs back inside, climbs on a stool, strains to look into the cup. "Is there a tomato yet?" Dad says, "No, not yet. We have to wait for a while." Down she scrambles, off she runs.

Daddy picks up the newspaper and begins to read. A few minutes later, here she comes again. She climbs on the stool, stands on tiptoe, and says, "I'm looking for the tomato." Her father says, "You had better forget about it. Go and play. It takes a long time for the seed to grow." She whines for a minute. Then she hears the television in the other room. Soon all is forgotten. Before you know it, a week has passed by. It turns into two weeks.

One day, she climbs up on her stool and sees the paper cup. "Daddy, come here! There's a tomato. When did it grow?"

Her wise father replies, "It grew when you stopped worrying about it."

What would it take for the kingdom of God to come? We have a list of a hundred things to do:

- Preach the gospel to all the nations
- Pray for the needs of world
- Listen to people with whom we disagree
- Teach the Bible to people of all ages
- Feed the hungry
- Make quilts for the homeless
- Speak out for peace in the community
- Bake brownies for the sake of justice
- Insist on forgiveness
- Welcome strangers to our supper tables
- Sing songs of joy and thanksgiving
- Keep God's commandments
- Give alms to the poor
- Build shelters for the downtrodden

All of these tasks are important things to do. They are important gospel seeds that Christians have a responsibility to sow. But ultimately it is God's responsibility to cultivate the beloved crop of the kingdom. As the apostle Paul once said of his ministry, "Neither the one who plants nor the one who waters is anything, but only God who gives the growth" (1 Corinthians 3:7).

When Jesus speaks of God's kingdom, he points to God's rule in all of life. There is a gracious governance to claim. Divine care is extended over the entire creation. All heaven waits for the creatures of earth to acknowledge God's generous dominion. The affirmation will not happen, except by the work of God taking root and bearing fruit. All we can do is sow the seed, then watch and wait. Then we give God the room to be God.

As Fred Craddock notes, the growth of the kingdom "takes place totally apart from human effort (for the sower sleeps and rises) and from human understanding ("the farmer does not know how"). The seed carries its own future in its bosom, and efforts to coerce and force growth are futile. The kingdom of God is exactly that: the kingdom *of God.*"[3]

There is a story about Angelo Roncalli, the Italian priest who became Pope John XXIII. It is reported that when he became Pope, John XXIII would end his prayers the same way every night. He would pray for the world, pray for the church, and pray for people.

He made his petitions with the authority of the Pope. Yet he would always conclude by saying, "But Angelo, Angelo, who governs the church? You or the Holy Spirit? . . . Very well, then. Go to sleep, Angelo."[4]

What is most striking about that story is not that Pope John withdrew from his work. No, he continued to pray and serve and sow the seeds of the gospel. He never withdrew from his work. But he was willing to let God be God.

---

1. As retold by Charles Rice at the annual meeting of "The Homiletical Feast," Princeton, NJ, January 1994.

2. Robert Farrar Capon, *The Parables of the Kingdom* (Grand Rapids: William B. Eerdmans Publishing Co., 1985), pp. 92-93.

3. Fred B. Craddock, *Preaching Through the Christian Year: Year B* (Valley Forge, PA: Trinity Press International, 1993), p. 311.

4. William H. Willimon, *What's Right with the Church* (San Francisco: Harper & Row, 1985), p. 48.

Shouting
At A Storm

The story of Jesus calming the storm has always been a favorite story of the church. It has prompted the writing of many hymns, such as "Jesus, Saviour, Pilot Me" and "Give to the Winds Thy Fears," to say nothing of the Navy Hymn and others. The story has also provided the church with a graphic symbol of who we are. When the World Council of Churches was formed, leaders sought a logo to identify the whole family of Christ. They drew a fishing boat with the cross as its mast. It was a good symbol. Christians are people who are in the same boat with Jesus. Our destiny is intertwined with his. Through baptism, we have been fished out of a sea of despair and destruction. Now we belong to Christ. We put our hands in the hand of the man who stilled the water.

Yet as familiar as this story has become, it continues to have a dark and mysterious quality. Try as we might to grasp its full meaning, the story slips out of our grip. In fact, I have known people who quickly jump to a conclusion about what the story means, only later to have all certainty battered about by wind and waves. The story pushes us into deep and murky water, to the boundary between faith and fear. Like the disciples, we are left to ask, "Who is this, that even the wind and sea obey him?"

It happened, as you know, on the Sea of Galilee. Jesus had begun to criss-cross that body of water, teaching and healing on different shores. He finished a full day of telling parables, and told his followers it was time to leave. It is typical, in Mark's Gospel, that Jesus will teach for a while and then withdraw. He will perform some kind acts of mercy and then he will disappear. If someone discovers who he is, or learns what he is up to, Jesus muzzles them and refuses to let them speak. According to Mark, Jesus Christ is a mystery. He will not be captured by a title or a nickname. He simply acts, then disappears, leaving people to wonder, "Who was that Masked Man?"

This time, the disciples are with him in the boat. A fierce storm sweeps in, threatening their lives. As the twelve shake Jesus awake, bellowing for help, there is no question what he does. This may be the only time in the entire Gospel of Mark when Jesus directly helps his disciples. Once in chapter one, he relieves Peter's mother-in-law of a headache, but that doesn't count. Apparently the disciples never asked for help, or he never offered, or he was too busy preaching to the multitudes and healing the crowds.

Now, however, his safety was at stake, which meant they were in trouble, too. Those in the boat grew nervous. They poked Jesus, shook him, and said with an emphatic (and nervous) voice, "Teacher, we're in trouble here. Aren't you going to wake up?" With that, a weary Savior blinked twice, rubbed the sand from his eyes, and said, "Ah, shut up!" The wind ceased. The water smoothed out like glass. And the disciples grew *really* nervous. "Who is this, that even the wind and the sea obey him?"

We know about the storms, don't we? Not just the little storms inside us, but the furious, full-scale storms *out there*. Even in a temperature-adjusted, climate-controlled world, there are bursts of fury within the natural world. Earthquakes shake human confidence. Rivers swell beyond their banks. Wind smashes our windows. Creation seems strangely indifferent to creature needs and comforts. A storm can explode with rage, and remind us how powerless we are.

On May 31, 1985, a tornado system touched down in the northwestern corner of Pennsylvania. The wind whipped at 250 miles-per-hour, tossing trees like matchsticks, throwing automobiles into the air, and killing fifteen people in two counties.

What should have been a Friday afternoon of relaxation turned into a weekend of horror.

The little town of Cooperstown, Pennsylvania, was in the direct path of a twister. A retired woman by the name of Isabella Stewart watched nervously as the low, black clouds blew in. The wind blew furiously. Suddenly a string of oak trees began to topple like dominos. The woman went for her car keys, but the wind was too wild to go outside. In a sheer act of panic, Mrs. Stewart reached for the only tangible means of comfort and order. She grabbed her purse. Then she sat in a chair and waited for the worst to happen.

Fortunately she did not lose her life, although her dog and cat were never seen again. The brief storm was devastating in a region that was already under economic distress. Over ten years later, Mrs. Stewart says, "Whenever I see a black storm cloud coming, I fall apart inside. You can't know quite how that feels unless you have been through it yourself."

No wonder that people in the first century identified the unruly powers of nature as *demonic* powers. A storm, particularly a storm at sea, seemed every bit as irrational as the forces that drove people out of their minds. You cannot reason with a tornado. You cannot negotiate with the wind and waves. It is true that the earth is nourished by rain sent from heaven above. But lightning bolts and furious winds are another thing altogether.

So they poked Jesus awake, and he screamed at the storm. The wind was fierce, but he was fiercer. Jesus shouted at the storm as if the clouds were possessed by a demon . . . because, after all, they were. The twelve wondered: If wind and sea should conspire to destroy, who is this that grants us safe haven?

> *Jesus, Saviour, pilot me over life's tempestuous sea;*
> *Unknown waves before me roll,*
> *hiding rock and treacherous shoal;*
> *Chart and compass come from thee: Jesus, Saviour, pilot me.*[1]

We know the storms, don't we? Not just the unmanageable storms out there, but the storms that rage inside us. Outer destruction breeds inner despair. A tempest outside can provoke a squall of fear. When a safe, predictable world comes unglued, so do we. We need some assurance to hold us together. We listen for a voice to silence the anguished cries for help.

They removed a tumor from a friend of mine before Thanksgiving one year. He bounded back, went to work, and immersed himself in Christmas preparations. By New Year's Eve, however, he found himself in New York's Sloan-Kettering Memorial Hospital, scheduled for a second surgery.

As nurses came to prepare him for surgery, family members were asked to leave. They said their good-byes. When the family had gone, and the nurses finished their work, suddenly the storm descended upon his soul. Up to this point, my friend had kept a stiff upper lip and taken everything with a kind of clinical detachment. Now he began to weep uncontrollably. He was terrified of a demon called cancer, a sinister force of nature over which he had no control. And he was afraid to face it alone.

He said, "As I sat there on that hospital bed, heaving and weeping like a fool, I felt a hand on my shoulder. And then another, and another. My brother had come back with the others. He began praying for me, and all of a sudden, as quickly as the storm had come, it vanished. It was as if Christ commanded, 'Peace! Be still!' And I was . . . like I'd never been before."

Throughout eight days of recovery in the hospital, my friend had plenty of time to reflect. What came to his mind again and again were all those verses of scripture that he had memorized in Sunday School. "God is my refuge and strength, an ever present help in time of trouble" (Psalm 46:1). "Yea, though I walk through the valley of the shadow of death, I shall fear no evil, for Thou art with me" (Psalm 23:4). These verses were more than comforting assurances; they became the means for conveying to him the presence of Christ.

"Sometimes I hear the distant rumblings of the storm," he says. "But I know two things. First, I'm not the only person in the boat; there is Another called Christ. Second, no matter how terrible the storm, I have not been set adrift."

Give to the winds thy fears; hope and be undismayed:
God hears thy sighs and counts thy tears,
God shall lift up thy head.[2]

We know the storms outside. We know the storms inside. "Why are you afraid?" asks Jesus. "Tell me, why are you so fearful?"

If I were one of the twelve, I would say, "Look, Lord, isn't it obvious? We are surrounded by powers we cannot control. This is a world of tornados and cancer and fear."

Jesus presses by asking, "Have you no faith?"

Again, I would respond, "Sure, we do. We cling to stories like this one. We trust there is a Savior who can overcome every force to hurt or destroy. We affirm he has the power. But when the One in whom we have the faith is snoring in the back of the boat, we wonder if faith in him will pull us through."

Who is this, who falls asleep while wind and wave pound into the boat? That may be the most troubling question. Whatever the storm, we want everything to always turn out okay. We want a happy ending for every disaster. We want a God who can remain accountable for our damages. In the wake of Hurricane Hugo, a radio commentator interviewed a man who lost everything in the storm. At one point, the man said, "If God's in charge, I'm angry. But if God's not in charge, I'm worried."

Yet Mark tells us that the God we meet in Jesus Christ will not be handcuffed by our assumptions or bound by our requests. He has the great capacity to be in charge, as he calms the storm. But he does not prevent the storm from happening. Neither does he abolish all storms everywhere. Instead the disciples have to shake him awake as waves splash into the boat. When Jesus finally stirs, he seems annoyed. It is not clear for a minute if he is shouting at the storm ("Peace!") or the disciples ("Be still!").

Who could this be? The scriptures say, "He who keeps you will not slumber. He who keeps Israel will neither slumber nor sleep" (Psalm 121:3-4). Yet if you discover Jesus snoring in the back of the boat, the very sight pushes faith to its extremity. Perhaps Mark thinks of this story as an object lesson for the sermon that Jesus had just given to that great crowd of people. In the language of his sermon, Jesus is like a sower casting seed upon the mixed soil of his audience. After a demanding day, he tells the disciples to push out to sea. He drifts off into slumber, and the scene looks suspiciously like one of the parables he told that day: "The kingdom of God is as if someone would scatter seed and go to sleep" (Mark 4:26-27). The sower sleeps, and trusts the result to an unseen benevolence at work within a fertile soil. At the crucial moment he wakens to see what kind of crop has taken root.

It was dusk when five of us went out on a boat on Cranberry Lake, in the Adirondack Mountains of New York. About four miles from the dock, a fierce storm blew in. The water turned black. The sky was full of lightning. A full tank of gas did not comfort the crew. Neither did a sufficient number of life jackets. In short, I had rarely been so terrified in my life. There's something unsettling about sitting in a small boat with an outboard motor in an electrical storm.

As the captain made a daring run for the dock, questions came to mind. Was it foolish to be out there? Yes, but the storm had come out of nowhere. Would we make it back alive? Probably, although at the moment it looked very risky. If we didn't make it back alive, would we land in some Safe Harbor? I wondered. I worried. At that moment, I could almost picture Jesus waking in the back of our boat. A weary Savior blinked twice and rubbed the sand away. Then he looked at me with blazing eyes, searching me to see if faith had taken root.

"Who then is this?" Who is this, who insists that we trust him as brutal storms pound against the boat? It is Jesus Christ. He is the One who reveals that nothing in all creation shall separate us from the love of God.

> *Fairest Lord Jesus, Ruler of all nature,*
> *O Thou of God to earth come down,*
> *Thee will I cherish, Thee will I honor,*
> *Thou, my soul's glory, joy, and crown.*[3]

---

1. Edward Hopper, "Jesus, Saviour, Pilot Me," *The Hymnbook* (Philadelphia: Presbyterian Church, 1955), p. 336.

2. Paul Gerhardt, "Give to the Wind Thy Fears," *The Presbyterian Hymnal* (Louisville: Westminster/John Knox Press, 1990), p. 286.

3. "Fairest Lord Jesus," *The Presbyterian Hymnal* (Louisville:Westminster/John Knox Press, 1990), p. 306.

Mark 5:21-43

Proper 8
Pentecost 6
Ordinary Time 13

Time Taken,
Life Restored

The woman had been sick for a very long time. So long, in fact, she didn't know what to do. She didn't know where to turn. Everybody suggested a different remedy, but none of them would work. She visited many physicians, but none of them could help. She stayed sick. As time passed, she grew worse. All those medical bills were bleeding her dry.

So when she heard Jesus was coming to town, she pushed her way through the crowd. She'd heard about him, of course. The last time he worked on this side of the sea, "he had cured many," says Mark. "All who had diseases pressed upon him to touch him."

Now it was her turn to get well. She pushed through the multitude, saying, "I don't need to talk to him. I don't need to bother him. I don't need to slow him down with a lot of bedside chatter. All I need to do is touch the edge of his garment. Then I will be made well." As we have heard, that is what happened.

Well, almost. Because, as we have also heard, two things went wrong. First, no sooner did she touch his clothes than Jesus spun around and said, "Who touched me?" Apparently he didn't let anybody get healed anonymously, much less this anonymous woman. "Who touched me?" Jesus said. He stood there, looking for her, scanning the crowd. He looked at every face: some of them eager, some curious, some confused. He kept looking until he saw her. And her anonymous touch became a conversation face-to-face.

83

She told him what she'd done. He said, "Daughter, faith has made you well. Go in peace. Be healed of your disease." It was a big moment for her. There she was, sick, desperate, and anonymous. And Jesus healed her, blessed her with his peace, and gave her the name "daughter."

What I want you to notice is Jesus *took the time* to do all of this. For twelve years, the woman heard the scriptures declare her "unclean" because of her hemorrhage. Jesus took the time to heal her and restore her to full status in the community. For twelve years, she had shuffled through her days without dignity. On the day she touched Jesus, he turned and treated her as a human being.

I want you to notice he took the time to speak with her, because I also want you to notice that, because he took time for the woman, he *ran out of time* for somebody else. He was late for a previous appointment. That's the second thing that went wrong. While Jesus was busy healing the woman who had been sick for twelve years, a sick twelve-year-old girl died.

Fortunately this sort of thing doesn't happen much in the Gospel of Mark. Jesus got interrupted from a healing by a healing. Jairus begged, "Please heal my daughter." He intended to make the young girl well by a touch and a word. On the way, however, Jesus was interrupted by a sick woman he called his daughter. She interrupted him with a touch and a word. And the daughter of Jairus died because Jesus ran out of time.

It must have been an embarrassing moment. Imagine how that pushy woman must have felt. The word of death came, says Mark, "while Jesus was still speaking" to her. She stood there, healed and whole. Refreshed for the first time in years. Yet because of her demand on Jesus, death came to somebody else. Imagine how that woman must have felt. She had been sick for twelve years. If only she had waited another fifteen minutes, Jesus could have healed the little girl first. Then the woman could have pushed to the front of the line to touch the edge of his garment. I mean, her timing was all wrong.

Not only that, it must have put Jesus in an uncomfortable spot. Picture the girl's father. Jairus insisted that Jesus come to his house and help. The man stood by patiently as Jesus paused along the way. He grew hopeful as Jesus restored the sick woman. Then came the message from his house: "Jairus, don't trouble the teacher any further. Your daughter is dead." In the face of such news, what should Jesus say? "Sorry, Jairus, I meant to heal your daughter, but I guess I got held up." No, he couldn't say that. It's a difficult dilemma. Jesus meant to heal one, instead healed another, and the first one died.

As you know, Jesus eventually went to the house and raised the little girl from the dead. But that merely suspends the problem; it doesn't solve it. Because we all know that for every person who ever gets healed of a disease, someone else will die. For every person who can push through the crowd to claim the power of Christ, somebody else stands close at hand, having just lost a daughter or son.

I guess we need to take some time away from the story to sort it out. Some people get well. Others do not. What can we say about that?

Sometimes the words fail us. Early in my ministry, I received a phone call from a seminary classmate. It was late and he sounded distraught. Among his hospital rounds, my friend had begun to visit a young boy from his church. The child had leukemia. There was nothing anybody could do. This minister was faithful through all the rapid stages of the disease. They became friends. They played checkers together. They shared an occasional meal.

When the end was near, they were alone in the hospital room, quietly sharing the evening. Suddenly the boy broke the silence. He said, "Reverend, I think I know why God isn't able to make me better."

"Why is that?" said my friend.

The boy said, "Because I think he's busy helping everybody else."

My friend said, "I left that room, got in the car, and drove around for a while. I didn't know what to say." What can we say? Some people get well; others do not.

The Gospel of Mark would probably say, "That is the way this world is." All the gospels agree Jesus was a healer. He restored life in the face of death. Some of the stories sound quite successful.

Luke says, "People came to hear him and to be healed of their diseases . . . and all in the crowd were trying to touch him, for power came out from him, and he healed all of them" (Luke 6:18-19). Matthew says, "Jesus cured every disease and every sickness among the people . . . They brought to him all the sick, those who were afflicted with various diseases and pains, demoniacs, epileptics, and paralytics, and he cured them" (Matthew 4:23-24).

By contrast, Mark adds a note of restraint. Mark says, "They brought to him all who were sick or possessed with demons. The whole city was gathered around the door. And he cured *many* who were sick" (Mark 1:32-34). Do you hear the difference? Jesus "cured many," not all. Many got well around him, but not everybody.

The Gospel of Mark knows what you and I know: sooner or later, one way or another, all of us become sick. The warranty runs out on our moveable parts. A stain appears on the X-ray. The blood count changes without warning. Or a hemorrhage begins and lasts twelve years. That's how it is in a world like this. Like it or not, sooner or later, one way or another, time will run out.

Sometimes the human body develops a problem that cannot be fixed, just like the daughter of Jairus. She died. Other times, somebody may stop the clock prematurely. That's what happened to Jesus. He was put to death on a tree. Like it or not, every human life will run its course.

One of the great illusions of our age is that we can live forever through better medicine. So we spend billions of dollars on medical research. We build machines that keep our lungs breathing. We design great drugs to keep our hearts ticking. Like that sick woman, we are willing to spend all that we have to clot up that hemorrhage. But we're not necessarily better for it. All we do is buy a little bit of time.

The writer of Mark starts with what we know: this is a world of sickness and death. Sooner or later, every single life runs out of time.

But Mark knows something else. Jesus came preaching, "The time is fulfilled; God's kingdom is near." And every sick person he touched became well, one person at a time. And every hopeless person who trusted his word found peace, one person at a time.

And do you know why? Because in Jesus Christ, the eternal realm of God has intersected our world of timelines and lifespans. In Jesus Christ, the God beyond time has intruded upon our business-as-usual. That is, even though Jesus didn't heal everybody, the day will come when he will. Even though he ran out of time, he will never run out of time. He was born, and raised, to redeem our days with the powerful touch of God's eternity. And that's the good news that makes all the difference.

So let's go back to the story . . . The messengers said, "Jairus, your daughter is dead. Don't trouble the teacher any more."

Jesus said, "Jairus, do not fear, only believe."

At the house, there was a great commotion with people weeping and wailing loudly. Jesus said, "Why do you make a great commotion? The child is not dead but sleeping." They laughed at him, because he didn't seem to know what kind of world this is.

Yet Jesus had the last laugh. He took the child by the hand and said, "Get up!" Immediately she got up, alive and well, and she began to walk.

In one of Flannery O'Connor's short stories, there is a character who speaks a great line. He says, "Jesus was the only One that ever raised the dead, and He shouldn't have done it. He has thrown everything off balance."[1] Indeed he has. A sick woman pushed through the crowd to touch the garment of Jesus. We could expect him to rebuke her and say, "Get out of my way." Or he could have ignored her because he was busy. Instead Jesus interrupted his work to do his work.

When the interruption caused Jairus to hear the sad news that his daughter was dead, we might have thought, "Well, that's that." At best, we could expect the tardy Jesus to make an apology. Or maybe we could ask him to lead the funeral service.

But Jesus has never led a funeral. Instead he presides over a resurrection. Thanks to Jesus, everything has been thrown off balance. The world as we know it is becoming "the kingdom of our Lord and of his Christ" (Revelation 11:15).

In the meantime, whenever any of us gets healed of a disease, we see a brief sign of God's kingdom still breaking in. Whenever a surgical procedure makes us well, we are reminded of a final destiny when all shall be well. Whenever we are saved from the jaws of death, it is a blessed disruption of the world as we know it. It is a glimpse of God's new creation, already present yet still coming through Jesus Christ our Lord.

We cannot be naive. We know what kind of world this can be. There are occasions when life cannot be saved or sustained. There are moments when it looks like Jesus our savior has run out of time.

But we also know Jesus Christ will never really run out of time. For the Lord is risen. He is stronger than every power that can damage, hurt, or destroy. And he will not cease his labor, until one by one, he takes each of us by the hand and raises us from the dead.

---

1. Flannery O'Connor, "A Good Man Is Hard to Find," *A Good Man Is Hard to Find and Other Stories* (New York: Harcourt Brace Jovanovich, Publishers, 1983), p. 28.

Mark 6:1-13 (C)   Proper 9
Mark 6:1-6 (L, RC)   Pentecost 7
Ordinary Time 14

Anybody Listening?

His name was George, and he sat in the back row of the sanctuary on the preacher's right. A permanent scowl was chiseled on his face. His posture announced to all that he was a man not easily pleased. Ushers tip-toed around him. Whenever his name came up in conversation around church hallways, someone would always ask, "Why does a grouch like that keep coming to worship?"

No one ever came up with an answer. One thing was certain — George was particularly hard on preachers. "I have heard hundreds of sermons over the years," he announced to his last pastor, "and I haven't heard many sermons I've liked." Some who sat near the back row wondered if George ever actually heard a sermon. Each week as the preacher began, they would inevitably hear a steady "click, click, click" from George's pew. If anyone nearby turned to identify the source, they might see a stained glass sunbeam reflecting from George's chrome-plated fingernail clippers.

"Preacher," George said at the narthex door one day, "I don't get much out of your sermons." Before he could restrain himself, the long-suffering minister blurted out, "I know, George. But at least you're getting a weekly manicure."

Is anybody listening? That's the question that haunts every preacher. Sometimes we preachers stand up in the pulpit, offer the fruits of careful study and thought, and wonder if anything is getting through. Other times we feel like the apostle Peter in the third

89

chapter of Acts, who said, "I have no silver or gold, but what I have I give you" (Acts 3:6). On the rare days when the words are tightly crafted, the logic is unusually clear, and the metaphors are finely tuned, a preacher may look out on one glazed-over face after another. On the more common days when the preacher's throat is parched, the head is pounding, and everybody might have been better off if the preacher had skipped worship and gone out for brunch, someone usually says, "Thank you for your words today; you were speaking to me." So today, I want to preach a sermon about sermons. I invite you to reflect with me on the curious business of Christian preaching.

Is anybody *listening*? That's a good question, because preaching is primarily an oral art. If people cannot speak, they cannot preach. Sermons, by definition, are aural events. Somebody speaks to people who come to hear something. The eternal gospel of God is entrusted to the vibration of words across the eardrum.

Most of us have known ministers who forget this. They hide behind footnotes and academic margins. Or they use fat, empty words to indicate they are smarter than everybody else. Or they glue their eyes to some gilded manuscript on the lofty pulpit, afraid to look at mere mortals down below. These preachers forget that preaching is a particular moment of talking to everyday folks in the context of worship. Woe to the preacher who forgets!

When Thomas Gillespie began his tenure as the president of Princeton Theological Seminary, he recalled the last time he spoke from the pulpit of the seminary chapel as a student thirty years before. It was preaching class and the occasion did not go well. At one point, an exasperated professor interrupted him to say, "Mr. Gillespie, if your name were not on this manuscript, I would have sworn that it had been written by George Adam Smith and preached to Queen Victoria. Mr. Gillespie, come down from your theological high horse and speak to Aunt Fannie in the front pew."[1] It was good advice. A preacher speaks to real people, present and accounted for, in the hope they will listen.

Of course, let's admit that not every sermon is worth hearing. On July 8, 1741, Jonathan Edwards preached a notorious sermon about the wrath of God. The title says it all: "Sinners in the Hands of an Angry God." Word spread about the sermon. Printed copies were widely distributed. When some people read it, they were glad they skipped worship that day. Isaac Watts, the hymn writer, was one of them. After he read a copy of the sermon, Watts scribbled a note in the margin. "A most terrible sermon, which should have had a word of Gospel at the end of it."[2]

Watts had a point. Every sermon, in some way or another, should proclaim good news. Christian preaching is not only speaking to folks in church; it is speaking the gospel, that extraordinary good news from God that breaks out in Jesus Christ. Jesus is the one sermon worth hearing. Every Christian preacher must keep that straight. Otherwise, a mist in the pulpit becomes a fog in the pew. Every Sunday, a piece at a time, it is the preacher's task to announce that Jesus Christ embodies the good news of God.

And yet, *is anybody listening?* That's the question in the story we heard this morning from the Gospel of Mark. Jesus himself went to preach to his hometown congregation, and as most who return home will tell you, it can be difficult to get a hearing. Imagine relatives and old neighbors crammed in the third pew, bursting with pride. A teacher from childhood peered through the cataracts and remembered "that cute little scamp." All four brothers wondered if episodes from family life would become sermon illustrations. In Mark's story, there is no mention of father Joseph. If Joseph was still in the picture, perhaps he was too embarrassed to admit publicly that the carpenter's kid grew up to be a preacher. Who knows if Mary came to listen? Perhaps she was busy giving one of her daughters directions for a homecoming reception after the service, telling her to inscribe a cake with the chocolate-frosted words, "WELCOME HOME, JESUS."

In any case, Jesus began to speak and "they took offense at him" (Mark 6:3). There he was, among his own people, surrounded by his own family, and they did not listen. Certainly he gave the same sermon he had preached from chapter one: "The time is fulfilled, the Kingdom of God is near at hand; repent and believe the good news" (Mark 1:15). As sermons go, it was solid, well-polished, and short. Yet nobody there had ears to hear him.

Then, as it happens frequently in the Gospel of Mark, Jesus told his followers to mimic what he had just done. He sent out the disciples, two by two. He said, "I'm going to give you the power to do what I've been doing. I want you to heal and confront evil wherever you find it. I give you authority to preach, although when you speak some people won't give you a hearing" (Mark 6:11). Isn't that striking? As Jesus sent his disciples with power and authority, he reminded them of the sure resistance to the words and deeds of God.

Anybody listening? Maybe not. Many people resist the opportunity to hear the good news. John Duckworth describes this preaching moment in a poem called, "Casey at the Pulpit,"

> *The smile is gone from Casey's lip; his notes are clenched in hand;*
> *He pounds with great intensity his fist upon the stand.*
> *And now he starts to make his point, and now he lets it flow,*
> *And afterward the people tell him, "Pastor, way to go!"*
> *Oh, somewhere in this favored land the Son is shining bright;*
> *The organ's playing somewhere, and somewhere hearts are light;*
> *And somewhere folks are learning, and somewhere Christians shout;*
> *But there is no growth in Mudville — Pastor Casey's been tuned out.*[3]

There are many reasons for such a scrambled signal. Some people are too familiar with the message, saying, "We've heard all of this before." Or, like the Galilee congregation, they might recognize the messenger all too well, observing, "This isn't anybody special. We know his family." Some people even develop routine expectations for Sunday worship. As a character in a play quipped, "Reverend, I didn't come to church to be preached to."

On the other hand, people can equally resist the gospel for reasons of unfamiliarity. They hear a new message and complain, "We never heard that before; is that in the Bible?" Or they create some distance with the messenger by saying, "She has a funny voice." Perhaps they blame an innovative setting, "Well, it was a strange worship service, after all."

Curiously, Mark says of Jesus, "He could do no deed of power there" (Mark 6:5). Jesus is the Strong Son of God, who came with power to plunder the house of evil. He came with the authority to inaugurate a whole new reign of God. Yet he could not perform miraculous deeds among people who did not listen to him. In the preaching of Jesus, as in all preaching done in his name, we catch a glimpse of the paradoxical power of God's kingdom. Jesus' work depends, to no small extent, on the capacity of people to receive his words. If they do not or cannot listen to him, Jesus refuses to coerce or overpower his hearers, for "he has no power from God to force the opponents to accept him, and in faithfulness to the rule of God he does not try to dominate them by ordinary means."[4]

So here's the question once again: *is anybody listening?* Hearing the good news is risky business. The word of God's reign can judge a person's commitments, undermine other allegiances, or rearrange someone's emotional furniture. The gospel may raise questions about private and public habits, commission people to serve in dangerous places, or speak difficult words to the thrones of power. No wonder, then, that someone once warned a gathering of pastors, "There are two kinds of sermons that people don't want to hear: bad sermons and good sermons."[5]

Do we really want to embrace the good news of the kingdom? It will require us to come prepared for worship. Those of us who are adults think we know what that means. We jump out of bed as if Sunday were another weekday, drink a quick cup of coffee, splash in the shower, iron some clothes, and rush around. If we are parents, we also steer kids away from the Sunday comics, wash behind dirty ears, tie stiff shoes, brush someone's hair in the face of certain opposition, and beg everybody to get into the car. It's hard work getting ready for worship!

But if we wish to claim a home in God's kingdom, we need to truly *get ready for worship*. What does that mean? It means to enter the sanctuary with a hungry heart, to whisper a prayer for God to speak even if people around us are speaking inanities, to tune into the prelude and let the kingdom's music drown out all other competing noises. What does it mean to get ready? It means to prepare for God in Christ to speak a word that could rearrange our lives. The Risen Lord speaks to us in the thick of our messy circumstances and tangled commitments, and he calls us to pick up a cross and get in step behind him, regardless of the cost. This is risky business for anyone with ears to hear. That's why so many people tune out. But if somebody should listen, and if God should get through, there's no telling what will happen.

Someone heard a sermon on September 20, 1989. The place was in the city of Pretoria, in the country of South Africa. On that September day, F. W. de Klerk was inaugurated as President of South Africa. Unlike leaders of many other nations at that time, de Klerk regularly went to church. No one in South Africa was surprised that, on the day of his inauguration, he invited his favorite pastor, a white man named Pieter Bingle, to lead a worship service in Pretoria.

Everybody gathered. The people sang some familiar hymns. They prayed well-polished prayers. Then Pastor Bingle stood up in the pulpit to speak. He based his sermon that day on the 23rd chapter of Jeremiah. As Bingle spoke, he said, "Mr. de Klerk, as our new President, you are standing in the council chamber of God. God is calling you to do his will. Today God calls you to serve as the President of South Africa. His commission is not to serve as the President of some of the people, but as the President of all the people of South Africa."

By the benediction, de Klerk was weeping. He called his family and friends together and said, "Pray for me. God has told me what I must do. And if I do it, I will be rejected by my own people. Pray for me, that I might do the will of God." Soon thereafter, de Klerk took steps to release Nelson Mandela. Then he began to negotiate with the African National Congress. Then he worked to dismantle the system of apartheid. The rest, as they say, is history.[6]

It happened because somebody listened to a sermon. Anybody listening?

---

1. Thomas W. Gillespie, "The Ministry of God," Opening Convocation, Princeton Theological Seminary, Princeton, NJ, 18 September 1983.

2. *Jonathan Edwards: Basic Writings*, ed. Ola Elizabeth Winslow (New York: The New American Library, Inc., 1966), pp. 150-167.

3. John Duckworth, *Joan 'N' the Whale* (Old Tappan, NJ: Fleming H. Revell Company, 1987), p. 101.

4. David Rhoads and Donald Michie, *Mark as Story: An Introduction to the Narrative of a Gospel* (Philadelphia: Fortress Press, 1982), p. 84.

5. I am indebted to Fred B. Craddock for this sobering advice.

6. As reported by Allister Sparks, "The Secret Revolution," *The New Yorker,* 11 April 1994, pp. 56-78.

Lectionary Preaching
After Pentecost

Virtually all pastors who make use of the sermons in this book will find their worship life and planning shaped by one of two lectionary series. Most mainline Protestant denominations, along with clergy of the Roman Catholic Church, have now approved — either for provisional or official use — the three-year Revised Common (Consensus) Lectionary. This family of denominations includes United Methodist, Presbyterian, United Church of Christ and Disciples of Christ. Recently the ELCA division of Lutheranism also began following the Revised Common Lectionary. This change has been reflected in the headings and scripture listings with each sermon in this book.

Roman Catholics and Lutheran divisions other than ELCA follow their own three-year cycle of texts. While there are divergences between the Revised Common and Roman Catholic/Lutheran systems, the gospel texts show striking parallels, with few text selections evidencing significant differences. Nearly all the gospel texts included in this book will, therefore, be applicable to worship and preaching planning for clergy following either lectionary.

A significant divergence does occur, however, in the method by which specific gospel texts are assigned to specific calendar days. The Revised Common and Roman Catholic Lectionaries accomplish this by counting backwards from Christ the King (Last Sunday after Pentecost), discarding "extra" texts from the front of the list: Lutherans (not using the Revised Common Lectionary) follow the opposite pattern, counting forward from The Holy Trinity, discarding "extra" texts at the end of the list.

The following index will aid the user of this book in matching the correct text to the correct Sunday during the Pentecost portion of the church year.

(Fixed dates do not pertain to Lutheran Lectionary)

Fixed Date Lectionaries *Revised Common (including ELCA)* and Roman Catholic	Lutheran Lectionary *Lutheran*
The Day of Pentecost	The Day of Pentecost
The Holy Trinity	The Holy Trinity
May 29-June 4 — Proper 4, Ordinary Time 9	Pentecost 2
June 5-11 — Proper 5, Ordinary Time 10	Pentecost 3

97

June 12-18 — Proper 6, Ordinary Time 11	Pentecost 4
June 19-25 — Proper 7, Ordinary Time 12	Pentecost 5
June 26-July 2 — Proper 8, Ordinary Time 13	Pentecost 6
July 3-9 — Proper 9, Ordinary Time 14	Pentecost 7
July 10-16 — Proper 10, Ordinary Time 15	Pentecost 8
July 17-23 — Proper 11, Ordinary Time 16	Pentecost 9
July 24-30 — Proper 12, Ordinary Time 17	Pentecost 10
July 31-Aug. 6 — Proper 13, Ordinary Time 18	Pentecost 11
Aug. 7-13 — Proper 14, Ordinary Time 19	Pentecost 12
Aug. 14-20 — Proper 15, Ordinary Time 20	Pentecost 13
Aug. 21-27 — Proper 16, Ordinary Time 21	Pentecost 14
Aug. 28-Sept. 3 — Proper 17, Ordinary Time 22	Pentecost 15
Sept. 4-10 — Proper 18, Ordinary Time 23	Pentecost 16
Sept. 11-17 — Proper 19, Ordinary Time 24	Pentecost 17
Sept. 18-24 — Proper 20, Ordinary Time 25	Pentecost 18
Sept. 25-Oct. 1 — Proper 21, Ordinary Time 26	Pentecost 19
Oct. 2-8 — Proper 22, Ordinary Time 27	Pentecost 20
Oct. 9-15 — Proper 23, Ordinary Time 28	Pentecost 21
Oct. 16-22 — Proper 24, Ordinary Time 29	Pentecost 22
Oct. 23-29 — Proper 25, Ordinary Time 30	Pentecost 23
Oct. 30-Nov. 5 — Proper 26, Ordinary Time 31	Pentecost 24
Nov. 6-12 — Proper 27, Ordinary Time 32	Pentecost 25
Nov. 13-19 — Proper 28, Ordinary Time 33	Pentecost 26
	Pentecost 27
Nov. 20-26 — Christ the King	Christ the King

Reformation Day (or last Sunday in October) is October 31 (Revised Common, Lutheran)

All Saints' Day (or first Sunday in November) is November 1 (Revised Common, Lutheran, Roman Catholic)

Books In This Cycle B Series

Gospel Set
God's Downward Mobility
Sermons For Advent, Christmas And Epiphany
John A. Stroman

Which Way To Jesus?
Sermons For Lent And Easter
Harry N. Huxhold

Water Won't Quench The Fire
Sermons For Pentecost (First Third)
William G. Carter

Fringe, Front And Center
Sermons For Pentecost (Middle Third)
George W. Hoyer

No Box Seats In The Kingdom
Sermons For Pentecost (Last Third)
William G. Carter

First Lesson Set
Light In The Land Of Shadows
Sermons For Advent, Christmas And Epiphany
Harold C. Warlick, Jr.

Times Of Refreshing
Sermons For Lent and Easter
E. Carver McGriff

Lyrics For The Centuries
Sermons For Pentecost (First Third)
Arthur H. Kolsti

No Particular Place To Go
Sermons For Pentecost (Middle Third)
Timothy J. Smith

When Trouble Comes!
Sermons For Pentecost (Last Third)
Zan W. Holmes, Jr.

www.ingramcontent.com/pod-product-compliance
Lightning Source LLC
Chambersburg PA
CBHW060131050426
42448CB00010B/2074